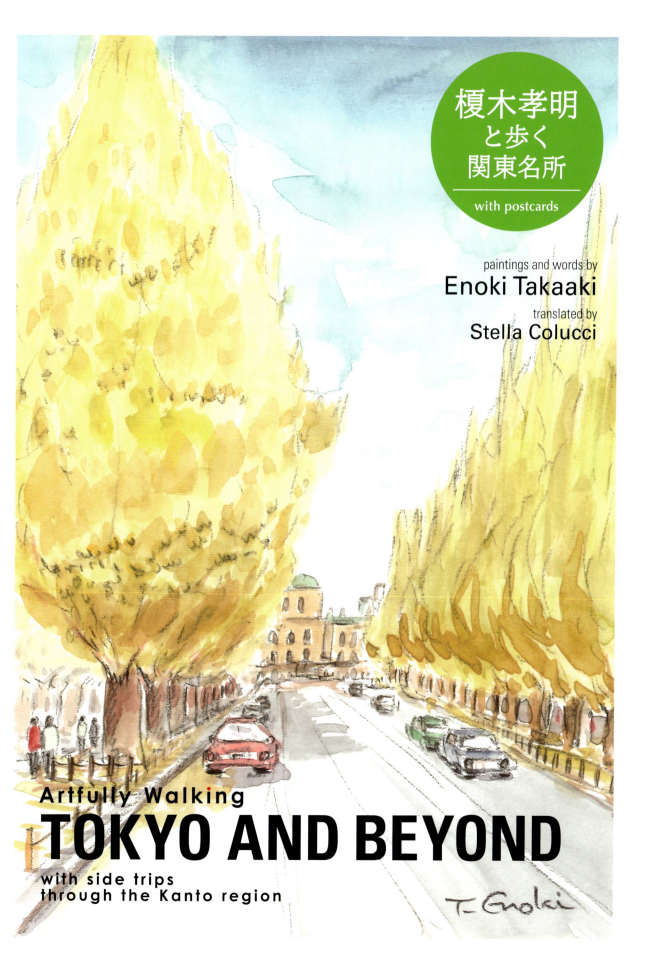

Artfully Walking
TOKYO AND BEYOND
with side trips through the Kanto region

Published and distributed by

MAMUKAI BOOKS GALLERY

3-14-19-6F Shibaura, Minato-ku, Tokyo 108-0023
+81 (50) 3555 7335
www.mamukai.com

Managing Editor	Yukako Kimura
Editorial Team	Takashi Kanazawa (ANNOVA)
	Asami Kishikawa, Aiko Kato,
	Harumi Ichimiya, Junko Yoshimoto
Design Team	Sankakusha Inc.
Contributors	Office Taka, Michiyo Yamamoto,
	Mark Bond, Amy Martinez
International Marketing	Arttrav Inc.

ISBN 978-4-904402-07-8
Cataloging in publication data: National Diet Library, Japan

Paintings and text copyright ©2016 by Enoki Takaaki
Translation copyright ©2016 by Stella Colucci
All rights reserved.

Printed in Japan

2 3 4 5 6 7 8 9 10

Disclaimer
While the author and publisher have made every effort to provide current information as of printing, things are always changing. If we missed something, please forgive us and let us know about it. The contents of this book are based on what we thought might be of interest to our international readers. It is our pleasure to share them to help make your travels more memorable. We hope *Artfully Walking Tokyo and Beyond* will serve as a practical guide for you to explore these places of wonderment, but please remember, this book is not intended as a substitute for professional travel advice. Any mention of specific products, services and/or establishments is for general information purposes and does not constitute an endorsement, paid or otherwise. The names of Japanese persons, including the author's, are written in the Japanese order of family name first. All of us sincerely thank you for your love and support for the *Artfully Walking* series!

本書は、アーティストが自身の目線で素晴らしいと感じた街を紹介することで、皆様にその良さを再認識していただいたり、旅や散歩の楽しみが広がることを願って制作しております。各施設へのアクセスや詳細情報は割愛させていただいている旨をご了承ください。
本書は2016年4月時点の情報をもとに編集しています。できるだけ最新で正確な情報を掲載するよう努めていますが、時間の経過とともに紹介した施設等に変更が出てくる場合もありますことをお含みおきの上でご利用ください。

postcards

postcard

初夏の日差し In That Summer Light ©Enoki Takaaki
Artfully Walking TOKYO AND BEYOND www.mamukai.com/tb/

postcard

天高く High into the Heavens ©Enoki Takaaki
Artfully Walking TOKYO AND BEYOND www.mamukai.com/tb/

cards

一葉の井戸 Old Well
©Enoki Takaaki

庚申塔と紫陽花
Koshinto and Hydrangeas
©Enoki Takaaki

水路の街（佐原）　Water Town (Sawara)　©Enoki Takaaki
Artfully Walking TOKYO AND BEYOND　www.marnukai.com/tb/

greeting card

遠い国から（横浜港） From Far, Far Away (Port of Yokohama) ©Enoki Takaaki
Artfully Walking TOKYO AND BEYOND www.mannukai.com/b/

はじめに

絵を描くことは、いつの間にか、私にとって息をするのと同じように"日常のこと"になっている。
けれども若い頃の私は、東京の風景を描かなかった。なぜなら東京は、私にとって無味乾燥な印象で、仕事の場ではあっても、絵の対象となる街ではなかったからだ。
ところが何度目かのインド旅行中に、ある心境の変化があって、ひと月ぶりに帰国した私の目に東京が今までと違って、輝いた景色に映った。おそらく心が俯瞰の目になって、宇宙から地球を見ることを知ったのだと思う。その目で見た東京は、ビルでさえ、人間ががんばって創った自然の一部のように思えて、いとおしさを感じるのだった。それ以来、東京のいろいろな景色を描き続けている。
今回、私にとって身近な東京と近郊のスケッチを、1冊にまとめてみた。きっとこの東京と同じように、ほかの国ほかの街にも、それぞれに輝いた景色が広がっているのだろうなあ、と思いながら。
おそらくこの広い宇宙で、一番美しい星は、この地球なのだと思う（私はまだ、宇宙の他の星には行ったことはないが）。その美しき地球を汚したり、同じ住人同士で傷つけ合ったりすることのおろかさを、私は絵を描き続けることで気づかされてきた。
美しい星には、素直な心と、美しい心が良く似合う。
そんな心で、この誌上散歩を、たっぷり楽しんでください。

榎木孝明

FOREWORD

Sketching has come to be routine for me, like breathing or eating. In my younger days, I did not draw scenes from Tokyo. It was my place of work, but it was not all that inspiring as a subject of art. During one of my trips to India, however, I had a spiritual experience that would change my perspective. When I returned to Japan after a month long absence, Tokyo looked very different. It sparkled. In my soul, I could "see" the Earth from the universe, as if I were given a bird's eye view. I came to cherish Tokyo, where even the buildings that people had so painstakingly built seemed to belong to the natural face of the Earth. Since then, I have been continuously painting the many landscapes of Tokyo. In this book, I have compiled sketches of some of the places in Tokyo and outlying areas that are familiar to me. Perhaps, just like Tokyo, there are sparkling landscapes that spread across other cities in other countries. I have not been to the other planets yet, but I bet Earth is the most beautiful planet in this whole universe. Sketching has helped me realize how senseless it is to spoil her, and to hurt fellow residents of this planet. Our beautiful planet Earth deserves a decent heart, a beautiful heart. I hope you enjoy a walk with me through these pages with those thoughts in mind.

Enoki takaaki

Artfully Walking **TOKYO AND BEYOND**

Step into my world of art (Postcards & Cards)
はじめに Foreword ·· 09

Central Tokyo

東京駅 Tokyo Station ··· 13
皇居 Imperial Palace ·· 14
日本橋 Nihonbashi ··· 15
銀座 The Ginza ·· 16
月島 Tsukishima ··· 18
国会議事堂 The National Diet ·· 19
東京タワー〜お台場 Tokyo Tower to Daiba ·································· 20
お台場〜浅草（隅田川めぐり）Daiba to Asakusa ···························· 22

Downtown Tokyo

浅草 Asakusa ··· 25
東京スカイツリー Tokyo Skytree ··· 26
蔵前・鳥越 Kuramae & Torigoe ·· 28
入谷 Iriya ··· 29
上野公園 Ueno Park ·· 30

Yamanote Circle

お茶の水 Ochanomizu ·· 33
本郷 Hongo ··· 34
椿山荘 Chinzanso ··· 35
四谷 Yotsuya ··· 36
新宿 Shinjuku ·· 37
ドコモタワー Docomo Tower ··· 38
明治神宮 Meiji Shrine ·· 40
神宮外苑いちょう並木 Gaien Gingkos ·· 41
恵比寿ガーデンプレイス Yebisu Garden Place ······························· 42
目黒川 Meguro River ··· 43

目次 CONTENTS

West of Tokyo

吉祥寺 Kichijoji ··· 45
小金井・立川 Koganei & Tachikawa ··· 46
秋川渓谷 Akigawa Gorge ··· 47
勝沼 Katsunuma ··· 48
河口湖 Lake Kawaguchi ··· 49

South of Tokyo

野毛 Noge ··· 51
多摩川 Tama River ··· 52
大井ふ頭 Oi Pier ··· 53
横浜 The Bluff at Yokohama ··· 54
北鎌倉 Kita-Kamakura ··· 55
鎌倉 Kamakura ··· 56
日本平 Nihondaira ··· 57

East of Tokyo

北千住 Kita-Senju ··· 59
柴又 Shibamata ··· 60
松戸 Matsudo ··· 61
成田 Narita ··· 62
銚子 Choshi ··· 63
佐原 Sawara ··· 64

North of Tokyo

川越 Kawagoe ··· 67
軽井沢 Karuizawa ··· 68
前橋 Maebashi ··· 69
那須塩原 Nasu-Shiobara ··· 70

A Few Words / Galleries ··· 71

本書では編集上の意図にそってエリア分けを行っております。
行政区画と異なる部分がありますことをご了承ください。

The editors acknowledge that the geographical organization of this book may not necessarily reflect official boundaries and jurisdictions.

Central
Tokyo

　東京で最も賑わいのあるエリア。高層ビルや再開発で新しく生まれた街だけでなく、江戸、明治、大正、昭和の建築や名跡も残る。東京湾沿いを歩けば、かつて海だったところが埋め立てられ、海岸線の地形はずいぶん様変わりしているが、多くの船が行き交ったであろう運河や橋には、今も現役で活躍しているものも多い。

The busiest area in Tokyo, the city center has managed to retain pockets of historical architecture and famous sites from the Edo, Meiji, Taisho and Showa Periods in spite of being reshaped by urban development and tall skyscrapers. Along Tokyo Bay, former landfills have been turned into a dramatically different shoreline. Canals and bridges, once used heavily by boats and ferries, continue to play an important role in Tokyo's waterways.

山手線 Yamanote Line
皇居 Imperial Palace
東京駅 Tokyo Station
国会議事堂 The National Diet
日本橋 Nihonbashi
月島 Tsukishima
銀座 The Ginza
東京タワー Tokyo Tower
お台場 Daiba
隅田川クルーズ Sumida River Cruise

東京駅 Tokyo Station

　現在の東京駅は、100周年を迎えるのを機に2012年にリニューアルされた。丸の内口駅舎は現代の建築技術を駆使して、ドーム型屋根や内部のレリーフなど創建時の仕様が再現された。東京駅には3つの出口があって、ひとつは日比谷・大手町に向かって高層ビルが整然と立ち並ぶ丸の内口。そして日本橋・銀座に向かう細い路地に昔ながらの店が連なる八重洲口と日本橋口。モダンな東京と歴史ある東京、二つの風景がここから広がる。私が出身地の鹿児島から上京して初めて降り立ったのもこの駅。特急「はやぶさ」（今は廃止になっている）で16時間の列車の旅の終着駅であった。期待と不安の入り混じった気持ちでホームに降りてから、すでに40年余り。ここは、私の東京での生活が始まった、旅立ちの駅舎でもある。

Tokyo Station went through major restorations to commemorate its 2012 centennial. Latest construction techniques were applied to recreate some of the missing bas relief pieces in the ceiling of the dome and in the interior sections. The co-existing facade of modern Tokyo and its traditional counterpart begins right here, where three exits lead out of the station. Tall skyscrapers line the modern landscape toward Hibiya and Otemachi from the Marunouchi Exit, while the Yaesu and Nihonbashi Exits take you to The Ginza and Nihonbashi through narrow side streets filled with older shops. I first arrived in Tokyo from my hometown Kagoshima at this train station. It was the end of the line after 16 hours (eight hours today!) on the super express *Hayabusa* that has since been decommissioned. I was anxious and full of anticipation when I got off that train some 40 years ago. This is where my life in Tokyo began, a New Beginning for me.

新たな旅立ち　A New Beginning

この"赤レンガ駅舎"が丸の内口のランドマーク。リニューアルで創業時の姿に復元された。
1914年の建設時は約74万人、100年後の再建時にも約78万人が携わったという。

The recently restored red brick train station is a landmark on the Marunouchi side. It took the hands of 740,000 people to build Tokyo Station in 1914. A hundred years later, 780,000 people were involved in the restoration.

皇居 Imperial Palace

東京駅の丸の内口からメインストリートをまっすぐ進むと、皇居に行きつく。都心とは思えない開放感で、季節にもよるが、皇居の濠を渡る風の、なんと心地良いこと。冬の渡りを諦めたらしい白鳥が、濠に1年中住みついていて、あたりを散策する人の目を楽しませている。その濠にかかる正門石橋（めがね橋）と正門鉄橋（二重橋）は、皇居巡りの定番コース。私も車で近くを通るたびに横目で橋を眺めていたが、ある時、観光客に混じって橋の前まで行ってみた。なるほど手前の橋と向こうの石垣が絶妙なバランスで、味わい深い雰囲気だ。人目も気にせず、さっそく1枚描いてみた。

めがね橋 Meganebashi

The main street from the Marunouchi Exit at Tokyo Station takes you straight to the Imperial Palace. Hard to believe there is so much space in the city. Seasonal breezes are very pleasant here. White birds quit migrating for the winter some time ago, nesting around the moat year round to amuse strollers exploring the area. A standard stop on a palace tour itinerary, the Stone Bridge is more commonly known as *Meganebashi*, and the Iron Bridge is called *Nijubashi*. The two bridges go across the moat side by side. I had been glancing at them every time I drove by in my car, but one day I actually walked up for a closer look along with some tourists. Only then did I notice that the stone walls in the back with the bridges in the foreground formed a striking balance, adding a lot of character. Not minding the people around, I just started drawing.

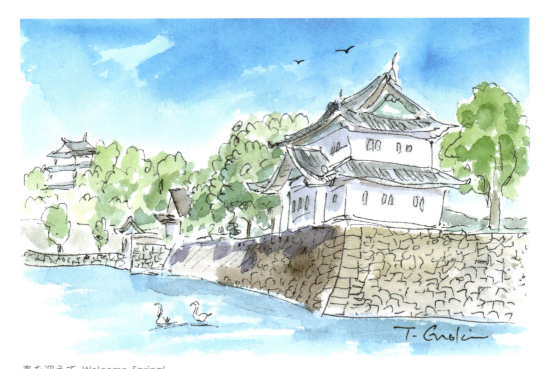

春を迎えて Welcome, Spring!
江戸城は日本史上で最も大きい城だった。石垣は何百年持ちこたえられるよう、石を加工して強度を考えながら積み上げられている。
Edo Castle was the largest castle in Japan's history. The walls of granite blocks were designed to last for centuries.

過去と未来
Past and Present

初代日本橋は1603年に架橋され、現在の橋は19代目。二重アーチ橋は重要文化財に指定。橋の欄干には見事な装飾が施されている。

The first Nihonbashi Bridge was constructed of wood in 1603. The current one is the 19th rendition. The double-arched bridge, with beautifully decorated railings, is an Important Cultural Property.

日本橋 Nihonbashi

　一見すると不思議な景色である。石造りの二重アーチの橋の上に、コンクリート造りの巨大な高速道路。日本橋は東京駅のほど近くにあり、日本の道路網の起点となっている（国道の距離はここを０地点として測定される）。橋の真上を首都高速が通ったのは、1964年の東京オリンピックの直前。景観よりも機能が重要視され、高度経済成長期のシンボルとなった。個人的にはいつかもう一度、この美しい二重橋の上に、青空が広がる景色を見てみたいと思う。

At first glance, it is a peculiar sight to see these concrete pillars supporting a modern highway directly above a double-arched bridge of stone. Nihonbashi (the bridge), the most famous bridge in Japan, is located in Nihonbashi (the district) close to Tokyo Station. Japan's national road network starts here at Kilometer Zero. The overhead highway was built during Tokyo's modernization program in preparation for the 1964 Olympics. Function over form, the unsightly view is a reminder of Japan's surge of postwar economic growth. Personally, I hope to see the unobstructed vista of clear blue skies over this classic beauty some day.

秘めたる時間 Secret Moments

江戸時代の人がこの景色を見たら何と言うだろう？ タイムスリップして聞いてみたい。

What would someone from the Edo Period think of this view? Sure would like to step back in time to find out.

銀座
The Ginza

　銀座は日本で最も華やかな繁華街。デパートや高級店が建ち並び、その周囲に古い建物も残っている。今から70年ほど前の戦争でこの一帯の大部分が焼けてしまったが、奇跡的に残った建物が今も人々に親しまれているのだ。そんな姿に出逢うと懐かしさを感じて、「ごくろうさま」と声を掛けたくなる。大通りから一歩入ると街路樹が連なり、葉色の変化から四季を感じとることもできる。時間や季節の移ろいを惜しみ、大切に思う。銀座はそんな楽しみ方ができる街だ。

晴天の歌舞伎座　Kabukiza on a Sunny Day

歌舞伎座の前で待ち合わせ、と言うと、おしゃれな気がしてくる。東京の観光名所になって久しいこの建物は、銀座の街並みの中でもひときわ異彩を放っている。近頃はチケットがなかなか手に入らないほど人気らしいが、気軽に一幕だけを観劇できる一幕見席は当日券で予約もいらない。

Arranging to meet in front of the Kabukiza Theatre can put you in a stylish mood. As one of the must-see tourist sites, the main theater remains a distinguished highlight of The Ginza in spite of its evolving surroundings. Lately, tickets to *Kabuki* shows have been hard to come by, but Single Act Tickets are available for same day purchase without reservations.

いにしえの思い出（大野屋總本店）
House of Yore

新富町にある「大野屋總本店」。足袋、和装雑貨を扱う店で、歌舞伎役者、能、狂言、舞踏家をはじめ、一般の人にも広く愛用されている。安永年間創業。建物は1920年代の建造。

Onoya is a specialty boutique for Japanese footwear (*tabi*) and *kimono* accessories, frequented by professionals in the fields of *Kabuki, Noh, Kyogen* and traditional dance (*Nihon buyo*). Popular among shoppers as well, the reputable store in Shintomicho has been in the same building since the 1920s; the business was established in the 1770s.

Tucked among the department stores and upscale boutiques of the most celebrated shopping district in Japan are some very old buildings. Most of them burned down during the war about seventy years ago, but some remain miraculously untouched and charming. I am overcome by a wave of nostalgia at their sight, and it makes me want to say, "Thanks for sticking around!" Step off the main avenues where side streets are lined with trees, and you can feel the seasons change as the leaves turn colors. Time passes, seasons change, wistfulness can set in. That's The Ginza.

新緑の街(並木通り)
Street Trees Budding

銀座の裏通りに入ると、緑の並木が続く。銀座の街路樹は通りによって、異なる種類の樹木が植えられている。並木通りはリンデン、みゆき通りはヒトツバタゴ、交詢社通りはトウカエデ、花椿通りはヤブツバキなど。

A continuous line of trees hem the side streets of The Ginza. Each street has a different type of tree: lindens along Namiki Street; Chinese fringe trees on Miyuki Street; Japanese maples on Kojunsha Street; and camellias along Hanatsubaki Street.

なごり秋(みゆき通り)
Lingering Fall (Miyuki Street)

ここは「銀座アスター」という老舗の中華料理店がある通り。よく来る通りだが、この日はやたら明るく見えた。それもそのはず、街路樹の銀杏の木が真黄色の葉を揺らせていたからだ。いつもの都会の景色が、一見、新鮮に見えた秋の日だった。

Home to the well-known Aster Chinese restaurant since 1925 is Miyuki Street. I come here often, but it looked especially bright one day. And as it should have, for the leaves on the gingko trees had turned completely golden! The cityscape was crisp on that autumn day.

月島 Tsukishima

　銀座一丁目から地下鉄（有楽町線）で2駅、月島は、昔ながらのもんじゃ焼き屋が軒を連ねる街だ。棟割長屋を中心に栄えてきた明治から昭和の雰囲気が、路地のそこかしこに残っている。大正10年に設置された警察庁最古の交番は、今も現役で街を見守り続ける。交番の近くのビルの奥には、月島観音が安置されている。○○ヒルズのような新しい東京の景色も悪くはないが、ひと昔前の情緒を感じさせる月島のような景色もいい。空が茜色に染まる頃に、もんじゃ焼きの匂いが街に漂う。こんな風情こそ大切に守って、次の世代にも伝えたいものだと思う。

Two stops on the metro from Ginza Itchome on the Yurakucho Line, Tsukishima is a town of many old-fashioned Japanese crepe (*monjayaki*) shops. Here is a neighborhood of row houses that has managed to preserve the charms of yesteryear from the Meiji to Showa Periods. The oldest police box, placed here in 1921, still guards the neighborhood. Deep within one of the buildings near the police box, the Goddess of Mercy (*Tsukishima Kannon*) is enshrined. The newer areas in Tokyo like the "Hills" neighborhoods are fine too, but that nostalgic look of Tsukishima makes me feel something deep inside. In that moment when the *monjayaki* smells begin to drift through the streets, just as the skies turn crimson at sunset, I long for the good ol' days and hope that scenes like this would be preserved for future generations to appreciate.

月島ストリート交番
The Police Box

大正ロマンの面影を残す交番の建物。もんじゃストリート（商店街）の真ん中にあり、月島警察署の西仲通地域安全センターとして、今も現役で活躍中。

The police box in the middle of Monja Street shopping strip is reminiscent of the romantic Taisho Era. It is an extension of the Tsukishima Police Station.

もんじゃの匂い Monja in the Air

もんじゃ焼きのルーツは、江戸末期から明治時代、子どもたちが、だしで溶いた生地で鉄板に文字を書きながら食べて覚えた「文字焼き」がはじまりとか。

Monjayaki originated in the 1800s as a learning tool for children who could not afford school supplies. With leftover broth and flour, shapes of letters were cooked on a hot grill.

国の象徴 Our Nation's Symbol

国会議事堂（参議院）の見学は、平日9〜16時までの決まった時間に行なわれる。本会議が開かれる時などを除いて、予約なしで当日受付が可能。10名以上の団体見学は要予約、英語ツアーは旅行会社で取り扱っている。

Take a tour of the House of Councillors between 9AM and 4PM, except when The Diet is in session. No advance reservations necessary. For groups of 10 or more, guided tours in English can be arranged through travel agencies.

国会議事堂 The National Diet

　国会議事堂の中を取材で細かく見せてもらったことがある。それはまさに昭和初期の日本の技術と芸術の粋を集めた、今も機能する美術館であった。1920年から17年の年月をかけて完成したという。日本全国から厳選して集められた建材や石材で、壁や床、内部の装飾が施された。議場の形式は、ドイツの影響を受けているらしい。平日に行くと、参議院の本会議場や中央広間の見学を受付で申し込むことができる。政治にあまり興味がない人も、試しに見学コースに行ってみると、日本の国について考えるきっかけを感じられるかもしれない。

When I did a story on the National Diet Building, I was given a detailed tour inside. It was a functional museum boasting a collection of Japanese art and technology from the early Showa Period. From the time they broke ground in 1920, it took 17 years to build. Natural stone and materials from all over Japan were carefully selected for the walls, floors and interior adornments. The architectural style was modeled after German design. If you go on a weekday, you can sign up at the reception desk for a free tour of the gallery and courtyard of the House of Councillors. Even without a keen interest in politics, taking the tour might trigger some thoughts about the way things are run in this country.

東京タワー〜お台場 Tokyo Tower to Daiba

　六本木から東京タワー、増上寺、浜離宮恩賜公園、お台場へ至るルートは、東京の昔ながらの光景と近代的な光景を一度に楽しめるコースだ。東京タワーは六本木や芝一帯から間近に望めるが、私が一番美しいと思うのは、麻布台3丁目の外交史料館前から望む構図である。将軍家ゆかりの増上寺や浜離宮恩賜庭園を散策しながら湾岸へ。新交通ゆりかもめに乗ってお台場に行くと、緑に彩られた入り江とレインボーブリッジが絵心を誘う。近代的なエリアながら、都内でこれほど大きな空が見られる場所もそうないだろう。

The walking course from Roppongi to Tokyo Tower, Zojoji Temple, Hama Rikyu Gardens and on to Daiba showcases a contrasting landscape of Tokyo past and present all around. You can see Tokyo Tower up close from Roppongi and Shiba, but the most beautiful composition for me is the view from the Archives of the Ministry of Foreign Affairs at Azabudai Sanchome. Explore Zojoji Temple and Hama Rikyu Gardens as you walk toward the bay. Ride the monorail to Daiba. The Rainbow Bridge and a picturesque green inlet will tug at your art sense. This new, modern part of Tokyo is actually one of the few places where you can see open skies.

**麻布台3丁目
(外交史料館前)
Azabudai
(MOFA Archives)**

スカイツリーができてから、東京一の高さは奪われてしまったが、私の中での存在感は、その名前が示す通り、やはり東京タワーが東京一だと思っている。

Tokyo Tower may have lost its claim to the Skytree as the tallest guy in town, but for me, it is still "The Tower of Tokyo," the Number One.

悠久の門（増上寺）
The Eternal Gate (Zojoji Temple)

増上寺は徳川家ゆかりの寺で、6人の将軍の墓がある。境内には「江戸三大名鐘」と呼ばれる鐘楼堂があり、江戸時代、この堂の鐘の音は遠くまで響いていたそうだ。今も朝夕鐘が撞かれる。大晦日に撞く除夜の鐘は108回で、108の煩悩を浄化する。

Zojoji was the family temple of the Tokugawa dynasty. Six of their shoguns are entombed in the mausoleum. One of the Three Great Temple Bells of Edo within the temple complex could be heard from long distances away during the Edo Period. The temple bell is still tolled twice a day, and on New Year's Eve, the bell tolls 108 times to keep us from straying toward the 108 earthly passions (*bonno*).

大名庭園（浜離宮恩賜公園）
Shogun Park (Hama Rikyu Gardens)

浜離宮恩賜公園は、いにしえの美しさを残す庭園でありながら、周辺の近代的なビルの姿も見渡せる。東京の新旧を比較する絶好の場所の一つである。昔将軍が鷹狩りをした地。この公園には1年を通して季節の花がいつも咲いている。

At Hama Rikyu Gardens, modern skyscrapers fill the skyline of a relic landscape; another perfect place to compare classic and modern Tokyo. Once upon a time, the Tokugawa shoguns hunted for ducks here. Something is blooming in the park all year round.

爽やかな季節（レインボーブリッジ）
A Refreshing Season (Rainbow Bridge)

浜離宮の最寄り駅、汐留から新交通ゆりかもめでお台場海浜公園へ。レインボーブリッジには徒歩で渡れる遊歩道があり、お台場からの帰りは、海の景色を見ながら芝浦ふ頭駅まで歩くのもいい。

Hop on the Yurikamome Line from Shiodome Station, the closest stop for Hama Rikyu, and get off at Odaiba Kaihin Koen. Use the pedestrian walkway to reach the Rainbow Bridge. Enjoy the ocean views as you walk to Shibaura Futo Station for the return trip from Daiba.

ゆりかもめ　Yurikamome Line

冬の晴れ間（お台場海浜公園）
The Winter Sun Peeks Through (Odaiba Marine Park)

お台場は東京湾岸に人工的に作られた島。TV局や科学館、複合レジャー施設などがあり、いろいろな楽しみ方ができる。

Sitting on an island of reclaimed land in Tokyo Bay, Daiba is loaded with fun things to see and do like TV production studios, science museums and entertainment facilities.

お台場〜浅草（隅田川めぐり）
Daiba to Asakusa (Sumida River Cruise)

　隅田川は江戸時代より物流を支えてきた河川。近年、船に乗って隅田川の名所を見物する「隅田川めぐり」が大変な人気になっている。お台場と浅草を結ぶクルーズでは、隅田川にかかる12の橋を巡る。お台場海浜公園を出発した船は、まず堂々たるアーチの勝鬨橋をくぐる。両岸にそびえ建つ高層マンション群を過ぎると、優美なデザインの中央大橋が見えてくる。赤穂浪士が渡ったことで知られる永代橋。稲穂の黄金色を象徴した蔵前橋。三連のアーチが美しい厩橋。青い大きなアーチを描く駒形橋。橋の一つひとつに時代の足跡がある。鮮やかな朱色の吾妻橋が、江戸東京の川を巡る小さな船旅の締めくくり。陸にあがれば、浅草見物が待っている。

勝鬨橋 Kachidoki-bashi

1940年に竣工した勝鬨橋は、当時の日本の最先端の技術と技量を誇った。当初は橋が跳開する可動橋として利用されていたが、水上交通の減少と陸運の発達で50年近く橋の開閉がなく、開かずの橋となっている。もう一度、橋をあげようという有志の活動が続いている。

Kachidoki-bashi was built in 1940. It demonstrated Japan's best technology and workmanship of the time. It was a functioning drawbridge at first, but it has remained closed for almost 50 years as automobiles gradually replaced water transport. Advocates have been campaigning for the drawbridge to operate once again.

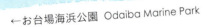
←お台場海浜公園 Odaiba Marine Park

勝鬨橋 Kachidoki-bashi

中央大橋 Chuo Ohashi

中央大橋 Chuo Ohashi

中央大橋は、お台場のレインボーブリッジと同日の1993年8月26日に竣工した。フランス人デザイナーによる主塔、欄干部分に日本の兜をイメージした意匠が施されている。橋の中央に建つブロンズ像はパリ市長からの贈り物。船の上からよく見える。

This stunning bridge was completed on the same day as the Rainbow Bridge in Daiba on August 26, 1993. A French design firm modeled the main pillar and suspension cables after a Japanese warrior's helmet (*kabuto*). The bronze statue in the middle of the bridge was a gift from the mayor of Paris. You can get a good look from the water bus.

Sumida River has been a major commercial transport route since the Edo Period. In recent years, river cruises have become a popular way to tour the famous sites along Sumida River, and the course between Asakusa and Daiba will take you under its twelve bridges. If you board the water bus from Odaiba Seaside Park (*Odaiba Kaihin Koen*), you will first go through the large archway of Kachidoki Bridge (*Kachidoki-bashi*). Once you pass the tall condo buildings lining the banks, the graceful architecture of the Chuo Ohashi comes into view. Eitai-bashi is especially famous for the 47 Ronin crossing it. Kuramae-bashi symbolizes golden sheaves of rice. Umaya-bashi has a triple arch, and Komagata-bashi forms a giant blue arch. Each bridge has its own footprint in time. The bright red Azuma-bashi signals the end of a small journey of Edo-Tokyo across the water. Continue ashore where a stroll through Asakusa waits.

永代橋 Eitai-bashi

永代橋は、5代将軍徳川綱吉の50歳を記念して1698年に敷設された。現在の永代橋は、関東大震災直後、東京で初めて耐震式の橋として架橋された。勝鬨橋とともに国の重要文化財となっている。

The original Eitai-bashi was built in 1698 to celebrate the fiftieth birthday of Shogun Tsunayoshi, the fifth Tokugawa ruler. The current bridge was rebuilt in 1926 as Tokyo's first earthquake-proof bridge after the original one collapsed in the Great Kanto Earthquake. This bridge and Kachidoki-bashi are both Important Cultural Properties.

P24 »

永代橋
Eitai-bashi

隅田川 Sumida River

蔵前橋
Kuramae-bashi

厩橋
Umaya-bashi

蔵前橋 Kuramae-bashi

蔵前橋は、欄干に「富士見の渡し」や力士のレリーフが飾られている。両国橋と蔵前橋の間は「隅田川テラスギャラリー」になっていて、防潮堤に錦絵などが展示されている。遊歩道もあり、散歩にもおすすめだ。

Artful designs featuring river crossings and sumo wrestlers were worked into the bridge railings of Kuramae-bashi. The Sumidagawa Terrace Gallery, between Ryogoku-bashi and Kuramae-bashi, displays Japanese woodblock prints by the seawall. The Terrace is a nice walking path.

厩橋 Umaya-bashi

厩橋の名称は、江戸時代、幕府の馬小屋・御厩があったことに由来する。橋のあちらこちらに、馬をモチーフにしたレリーフがある。橋のたもとに祀られているのは「厩橋地蔵尊」。地域の人々に親しまれている地蔵堂だ。

The images of horses on Umaya-bashi are a reminder that the bridge was named after the former site of the Tokugawa government's stables. At the foot of the bridge is the Umaya-bashi *Jizo*, dear in the hearts of locals. The *jizo* protects children and voyagers.

Downtown
Tokyo

　上野、浅草を中心とした下町エリアは、老舗や神社、仏閣、古い民家が、それこそひしめき合うように建っている。東京スカイツリーができてから、下町のどこからでも見えるこのタワーを、どうやって絵の構図に入れようかと考える楽しみが増えた。人にもよるだろうが、私は高いところから見下ろす景色より、見上げる景色が好きである。

Downtown Tokyo is a tightly squeezed group of neighborhoods full of well-established shops, shrines, temples and age-old homes concentrated around Ueno and Asakusa. Ever since the Skytree went up, looking for different compositions to draw this tall figure has become another form of amusement for me. You can see it no matter where you are downtown. It depends on the person, I am sure, but I prefer the low-angle perspective of looking up as opposed to looking down upon a landscape.

上野 Ueno　　入谷 Iriya　　浅草 Asakusa　　吾妻橋 Azuma-bashi
蔵前・鳥越 Kuramae & Torigoe　　駒形橋 Komagata-bashi　　東京スカイツリー Tokyo Skytree

駒形橋　Komagata-bashi

駒形橋の近隣にはどじょう鍋やうなぎ、むぎとろ、やぶそばなど江戸の味の老舗が並ぶ。この橋の途中には隅田川を一望できるバルコニーがあって、そこからの眺めも美しい。

Around Komagata-bashi are many well-established restaurants serving authentic Edo favorites, such as hot pots with fresh-water loach (*dojo nabe*), grilled eels (*unagi*), grated yam (*mugitoro*) and buckwheat noodles (*yabu soba*). Enjoy beautiful views of Sumida River from the overlook perch on the bridge.

吾妻橋　Azuma-bashi

隅田川めぐりのゴールとなる吾妻橋。春には隅田川沿いに美しく咲く桜が、吾妻橋の朱色を一層華やかに引き立てる。橋の向こうに見える金色のオブジェは「flamme d'or 金の炎」。吾妻橋の船着き場から少し歩くと東京スカイツリー、吾妻橋を渡ると浅草寺や仲見世がある。

Azuma-bashi marks the end of the river cruise. Cherry blossoms help the red bridge stand out even more in spring. On the other side is the golden Asahi Flame (Flamme D'or). A short walk from the pier leads to the Tokyo Skytree. Cross the bridge to reach Sensoji Temple and the shops at Nakamise.

にぎわいの時(雷門)
A Gathering

浅草 Asakusa

　雷門の赤い大提灯の前はいつも賑わっている。東京にどんなに新しい観光名所ができようと、この超A級の名所は他の追従を許さない。私もここに来るたびに、なんだか懐かしくて嬉しくなる。照れくさい話ではあるが、私が初めてここに来たのは40年前、田舎から母が上京してきた時だった。当時、私はまだ東京の地理にうとく、ひとまず観光バス(はとバス)に乗ろうということになった。皇居、明治神宮、浅草と巡る半日コースだったが、意外と充実していて面白かったのを覚えている。雷門は今もバス観光の目玉らしい。

雷門には風神(風をつかさどる神様)と雷神(雷をつかさどる神様)が祀られている。門に向かって右側が風神、左側が雷神。水をつかさどる龍神も祀られていて、大提灯の下に龍の彫刻があり、雷門をくぐって右側に金龍像、左側に天龍像がある。

Kaminarimon is flanked by the Wind God (*Fujin*) on the right and the Thunder God (*Raijin*) on the left. The Gods of Water are also enshrined. Look under the lantern for the Dragon Sculpture (*Ryujin*). On the back side of the gate, the female Golden Dragon (*Kinryu*) and the male Heavenly Dragon (*Tenryu*) keep stormy seas under control.

It is always crowded in front of the giant red lantern at The Thunder Gate (*Kaminarimon*). No matter how many new famous places are built in Tokyo, this A-1 tourist attraction will never be second best. Every time I come here, it reminds me of things that make me smile. I am embarrassed to tell you about my first time here 40 years ago. I was not yet familiar with the city when my mother came to visit me from home, so we decided to take a Hato Bus tour. I recall that the half-day itinerary covering the Imperial Palace, Meiji Shrine and Asakusa was interesting and fun. Kaminarimon still seems to be the highlight of Tokyo bus tours.

下町のシンボル
(伝法院通り)
Downtown Symbol

浅草の伝法院通りから望むスカイツリー。伝統と新しさが共存するこの町で、そびえ立つタワーの光景がなじんでいる。

The Tokyo Skytree as viewed from Denpoin Street. This tower is becoming a familiar sight in a town where the old and the new converge.

東京スカイツリー
Tokyo Skytree

　下町を歩いていて、スカイツリーがビルの谷間から見えると、つい絵にしたくなる。隅田川、常夜灯、高速道路、スカイツリー。一見ばらばらのものが、微妙にほどよいバランスで、一枚の絵の中に収まる楽しみがある。みんなもきっと自分のお気に入りのスカイツリーの構図があるに違いない。私が好きなのは、川を入れ込んだ景色である。水辺はなんだか心をほっとさせてくれるからだ。それから雨上がりのスカイツリーもいい。雨が降っている時は、雲にはばまれて見えないスカイツリーの上部が、雨が上がって雲が晴れてくると、予想したよりもっと高いところまで、その光がのびていたりする。その景色に妙に感激するのは、私だけだろうか。

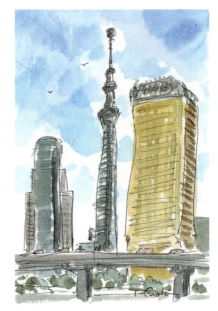

雨あがりの空（浅草）
After the Rain

浅草の隅田公園側から見た景色。首都高速、スカイツリー、アサヒビールタワーの構図が面白い。

This landscape is from Sumida Park in Asakusa. The Shuto Expressway, Skytree and Asahi Beer Tower form an interesting composition.

夕暮れて（隅田川） At Sunset

こちらも隅田公園側から、隅田川をはさんで眺めるスカイツリー。スカイツリーができてから、描きたい水辺の景色がずいぶん増えたように思う。634mの高さがあるので、いろいろな所からその姿を目にすることができる。構造のヒントは法隆寺の五重塔だという。

Here is the Skytree from Sumida Park again, from the other side of Sumida River. I seem to be drawn to water views ever since the Skytree was built. Reaching 634m high, it can be seen from many different places. The Skytree was modeled after the five-story pagoda at Horyuji Temple in Kyoto.

ビルの谷間から(錦糸町)
Between Buildings

錦糸町駅北口のアルカキット錦糸町前の通りに立つと、ビルとビルの間に巨大なスカイツリーが現れる。思いがけずこんなユニークな景色に出逢えるのも、街歩きの楽しみだ。

If you stand on the street in front of the Arcakit shopping center near the North Exit of Kinshicho station, the Skytree appears huge between buildings. Part of the fun of walking around downtown is coming across such unique landscapes.

Whenever I take a walk downtown and see the Skytree between buildings, I want to stop and make that sketch. Sumida River, streetlights, highways, the Skytree; at first these things appear disconnected, but they curiously offset each other, and waiting to see how they come together in a single painting is quite amusing. Perhaps everyone has a favorite composition for portraying the Skytree. Mine is to include the river because the waterfront has a soothing effect. So does the Skytree after the rain. Clouds hide the top section while it is raining. When the clouds disperse afterwards, the light reaches up the Skytree much higher than expected. I wonder if only I am strangely touched by that view.

春を待ちわびて
(江戸川区 新川 櫓橋)
Longing for Spring

江戸川区の新川に架かる櫓橋から見たスカイツリー。火の見やぐらの先に高速道路とスカイツリーが望める。

Standing at Yagura-bashi, the bridge that crosses Shinkawa River in Edogawa Ward, you can see the expressway and the Skytree past the watch tower that was once a fire lookout.

鳥越神社
Torigoe Shrine

鳥越神社は、約1360年の歴史を誇る。毎年6月の例大祭ではクライマックスの夜まつりで大神輿の練り歩きが行なわれ、数万人の人出で賑わう。

Torigoe Shrine dates back to the 7th Century. Tens of thousands of people crowd the streets during the shrine festival (*Reitaisai*) in June every year to see the heaviest portable shrine (*mikoshi*) paraded through during the day, then put back into storage at night with a climactic ending.

蔵前・鳥越 Kuramae & Torigoe

時代とともに様変わりする東京の街並みの中で、変わらぬ姿を留める神社・仏閣。昭和の佇まいが残り、近年クリエイターに人気のこの界隈で、よく知られているのが鳥越神社と蔵前神社だ。鳥越神社の威風堂々とした社は、私の絵にもってこいの風情である。蔵前神社は、住宅街にぱっと現れる赤い鳥居に目を惹かれる。よく山道や路地を歩いていて、突然、視界に赤い鳥居が飛び込んできて、ドキリとする時がある。蔵前神社もそうだった。しかし絵を描く者には、ひときわ目の覚める赤い色は、景色の中の絶好のポイントになる。

Though Tokyo's cityscape keeps changing with the times, shrines and temples remain constant. The Kuramae-Torigoe area has maintained that Showa look, attracting creative artists in recent years. The shrines are well known around here. I find that the dignified appearance of Torigoe Shrine makes an excellent subject for my sketches. Kuramae Shrine has a red *torii* gate that stands out in the middle of a residential neighborhood. It is eye-catching. Often, when I walk along the road or a mountain path, a *torii* will suddenly enter my range of view, startling me. I had that very experience at Kuramae Shrine. For an artist, that vivid red color can create the perfect focal point in a landscape.

蔵前神社 Kuramae Shrine

1757（宝暦7）年の勧進相撲から、相撲との縁がある蔵前神社。境内には満願成就で人間になったという落語の演目にちなんだ、真っ白い犬「元犬」の像がある。

Kuramae Shrine has long been associated with *sumo* wrestling ever since fundraising tournaments (*kanjin sumo*) were held here in 1757. The statue of the white dog comes from a classic oratory comedy (*rakugo*) about *moto inu*, who remained on all fours, stark naked, even after his wish to become human was granted.

入谷 Iriya

　入谷は東に浅草、西に上野と隣り合わせる街。入谷鬼子母神（真源寺）と、入谷朝顔まつりでよく知られている。鬼子母神は安産・子育ての神様として、日本で広く信仰されている神様。もとは人間の子どもをさらって食べてしまう凶暴な悪神だったが、釈迦に説かれて改心し、善神になったという云われがある。散歩や帰宅の途中に立ち寄るのだろうか、通りすがりの人々が鬼子母神の前で手を合わせる姿が、この街の日常のひとコマになっている。たまに長い間祈り続けている人を見ると、深い悩みごとでもあるのだろうかと、よけいな詮索をしてしまう。この境内で毎年7月に行われる入谷朝顔まつりは、下町の風物詩。寺院前の言問通りにかけて百数十軒もの朝顔の露店が並ぶ。

Iriya is a town sandwiched between Asakusa to the East and Ueno to the West, known for the Goddess Kishimojin and the Morning Glory Festival, both at Shingenji Temple. Protector of safe childbirth and the well-being of children, Kishimojin (Hariti in Sanskrit) was not always a benevolent goddess. According to myth, she abducted and devoured other people's children, and fed them to her own. With Buddha's teaching, she reformed and received healing powers. It seems routine for passersby to stop and pray here. Sometimes their prayers last a long time. I don't mean to pry, but it makes me wonder what might be troubling them. The Morning Glory Festival is held on the temple grounds in July. Hundreds of vendors set up shop to sell potted morning glories.

入谷鬼子母神 Iriya Kishimojin

日本には、願いを叶えたい時、困った時、悲しい時、せつない時、恐ろしい時などに神仏に祈る「神頼み」の習慣がある。鬼子母神が右手に持つ柘榴の実には、子孫繁栄の願いが込められている。

In Japan, we have a custom of putting our hands together—in hopefulness, more than in prayer, actually—in distress, in sorrow, in anguish, in fear; or maybe just to make a wish (*kami danomi*). The pomegranate in Kishimojin's hand, a symbol of fertility, bears the wish of those who seek many children.

上野公園 Ueno Park

　P31の景色は、上野恩賜公園にある「上野精養軒」のテラスから眺めたもの。上野精養軒は明治時代に開業し、夏目漱石や森鷗外など多くの文豪も通ったフランス料理店だ。中央に見える八角形の建物は、不忍池弁天堂。当時、遠くのビル群はなかったにしても、池の周囲の緑はきっと今と似た景観だっただろうと思うと、筆をとる手も快活に動き出す。弁天堂の近くに上野動物園がある。明治15年開園の日本最古の動物園。戦火の時代は悲しい歴史を刻み、昭和の高度成長期にはジャイアントパンダブームで日本中を沸かせた。園内には約400種の動物がいるが、今もパンダは一番人気のようだ。

The views on Page 31 are those from the terrace at the Seiyoken in Ueno. Natsume Soseki and Mori Ogai were among the many literary giants who frequented this French restaurant that opened during the Meiji Period. The octagonal structure in the center is Bentendo Temple at Shinobazu Pond. The cluster of buildings in the distance may not have existed then, but the natural landscape around the pond must have looked similar to what it is today. That inspires me, and the pen in my hand begins to flow freely. Near Bentendo is Ueno Zoo, the oldest in Japan since 1882. The Giant Panda stirred up a national craze during the 1970s and 1980s when Japan became an economic superpower. Decades earlier, the zoo had gone through bleak conditions in wartime. There are more than 400 types of animals today, but the Giant Panda is still the most popular attraction.

ゴリラ Gorilla

象 Elephants

ラマ Llama

パンダ Giant Panda

フラミンゴ Flamingo

上野動物園の動物たち
Friends at the Zoo

上野動物園で出逢った動物たち。上野動物園では、明治15年に日本初の水族館、観魚室も公開された。

Here are some of the animals from Ueno Zoo. The first aquarium in Japan was also built here in 1882.

上野 Ueno

弁天堂は七福神の唯一の女神、弁財天が祀られ、開運厄除け、芸能にご利益あり。池のあらゆる角度から見えるように、八角形に建てられている。

Benzaiten, the only goddess among the Seven Gods of Fortune (*Shichifukujin*), is enshrined at Bentendo Temple. She brings good fortune and prosperity to the arts. Bentendo was built as an octagon so it could be viewed from every direction.

見晴らしの場所
The Overlook

上野精養軒から見た景色。上野公園の高台に建っているので、森の向こうも遠くまで見渡せる。

Perched on a mound in Ueno Park, the views from Seiyoken restaurant extend way beyond the forest.

Yamanote Circle

　都心でありながら緑が多く、いろいろな場所で季節の景観に出逢うことができる。四季を身近に感じたいなら、気持ちに余裕を持って自然を見るといい。たった１本の街路樹でも、春の新緑、夏の深緑、秋の紅葉、冬の落葉と、それぞれに繊細な表情を見せてくれる。ときに東京にいることを忘れてしまうような、オアシス的な場所との出逢いもある。

This area is in the heart of the city, yet there is so much green space with seasonal landscapes in various places. If you want to feel close to nature, it is important to embrace it. Even a single tree can show particular expressions: spring green, summer radiance, fall foliage and winter leaves on the ground. When you come across a space that provides refuge, you could almost forget you are in Tokyo.

ニコライ堂 Nikolaido

ニコライ堂はイギリスの建築家、ジョサイア・コンドルが設計に携わり、1891年に竣工したビザンティン様式の教会。関東大震災で建物が大破し、1929年に再建して現在の建物になった。毎日13〜16時（10月〜3月までは15時半）まで拝観できる。

Nikolaido was designed in the Byzantine style by Meiji-era architect Josiah Condor. Originally constructed in 1891, the cathedral sustained major damages from the Great Kanto Earthquake and was rebuilt in 1929. Open daily from 13:00 to 16:00 (15:30 October to March) and during services.

お茶の水 Ochanomizu

　JR御茶ノ水駅と神田川をはさんで、北側に神田明神、南側に東京復活大聖堂（ニコライ堂）がある。私は都内に思い出の神社仏閣がいくつかあって、神田明神もその一つ。若い頃、出演した映画がヒットしますように、と祈願に訪れた神社である。商売の神様として有名で、江戸時代には「江戸総鎮守」として、将軍から庶民まで江戸の人々に広く崇められていた。かたやニコライ堂は、キリスト教の正教会（ギリシャ正教）の教会である。中央に大きなドームが設けられ、窓が小さく壁が厚い。なんとも目をひく建築物である。ギリシャ正教は日本ではあまりなじみがないが、日本人は外来のものにきわめて寛容な心を持つ。今ではここは御茶ノ水の一つの顔ともいうべき景色になっている。

Ochanomizu train station and Kanda River are nestled between Kanda Shrine (*Kanda Myojin*) to the North and Nikolaido to the South. Kanda Myojin is on my list of memorable shrines and temples in Tokyo. As a young actor, I came here to wish for my movie to be a hit. Famous as the patron god of prosperity in business, it was widely worshipped during the Edo Period by all classes of people, from the shogun to the masses, when it served as the all-embracing protector of the old capital. And then there is the Holy Resurrection Cathedral, affectionately known as Nikolaido, which belongs to the Autonomous Orthodox Church of Japan. An architectural marvel, it has small windows on thick walls topped by a central dome. Although the Japanese are not too familiar with the Orthodox religion, they are nonetheless quite receptive to things foreign. Today, this view is very much a permanent fixture of Ochanomizu.

神田明神 Kanda Myojin

「神田祭」で知られる神社。社殿の裏には江戸神社、水神社、だいこく様、えびす様などが祀られている。八百万の神を崇め、折々にあちらこちらに祈るのは人間の身勝手に思えなくもないが、人智を超えた存在を暗黙のうちに認めるのは、これはこれで日本の立派な文化であろう。

Known for the Kanda Festival, Kanda Myojin is actually a complex of enshrined gods and smaller shrines: two of the Seven Gods of Fortune (*Daikoku and Ebisu*), Edo Shrine and Water Shrine (*Sui Jinja*). Maybe it is selfish to pray here and there to a deity (*kami*) we find everywhere and in everything (*yaoyorozu no kami*), but the implicit recognition of a supernatural existence is, proudly, part of our culture.

本郷 Hongo

　どっしりとした赤い柱に、切妻造本瓦葺きの屋根。東京大学の本郷キャンパスにある「赤門」は、山の手の名所であり、小説にもときどき登場する。江戸時代には加賀藩の立派な大名屋敷だったらしく、私には敷居が高い気がしていた。だが実際に訪れてみると、地元の人々がよく行き来をしていて、本郷の街にずっとなじんできた門だとわかった。キャンパスには加賀屋敷時代に造られた、「心」という字を形どった池（三四郎池）もあり、学生や地元の人がのんびり散歩している。銀杏並木が色づく初冬の日差しの中で、赤門の朱色がふんわりと浮かび上がって見え、心なしか温かく思えてきた。

Interlocking clay tiles (*kawara yane*) form the roof that crowns a pair of thick pillars painted in vermillion. This is none other than the Red Gate (*Akamon*) of the University of Tokyo's Hongo Campus, a famous site that has made its way into several novels. Located within the beltway formed by the JR Yamanote train line, Akamon was part of the former Kaga *daimyo* estate. For the longest time, I thought of it as a formidable passageway, until I discovered upon my visit that the local residents were also passing through this neighborhood icon on a regular basis. On campus, students and locals take walks near Sanshiro Pond (*Sanshiro Ike*), shaped in the kanji character *kokoro* by the former occupants of the estate. On an early winter day, the gingko trees were faintly tipped in gold, and I felt a heartwarming moment when I saw Akamon in a red haze floating above gentle shafts of sunlight.

冬の日差し In the Winter Light

赤門の正式名称は「旧加賀屋敷御守殿門」。1827年、11代将軍徳川家斉の娘が加賀藩主のもとへ嫁ぐ際に、姫様の専用門として建てられた。かつてこの一帯は大名屋敷で、水戸藩や富山藩の屋敷も近くにあった。

Akamon is a nickname; its official name is "The Gate for Her Royal Highness at the Former Kaga Estate." It was originally built in 1827 for a Tokugawa princess bride so she could enter her new home in style when she married the Lord of Kaga. The campus and its environs sit on former *daimyo* estates of the heads of the Kaga, Mito and Toyama feudal provinces.

ある晴れた日に One Sunny Day

圓通閣は、大正時代に広島県の篁山竹林寺(たかむらさんちくりんじ)から移築されたもの。建築様式から室町時代末期の作と推定される。

Entsukaku was moved from the Chikurinji Temple in Hiroshima during the Taisho Era (1912-1926). Based on the architectural style that marries traditional Japanese construction with elements of Zen, historians estimate the three-story pagoda was built toward the end of the Muromachi Period (1392-1573).

椿山荘 Chinzanso

　椿山荘はかつて、椿が自生する景勝の地「つばきやま」だったという。明治時代に山縣有朋が邸宅と庭園を造ったのがはじまりで、戦後に式場、ホテルとなった。現在は「ホテル椿山荘東京」として各国の要人を迎え、国際会議も多く開かれる。台地と谷の起伏を巧みに利用した庭園では、春の桜、夏の深緑、秋の紅葉、冬の侘助と、日本の四季が堪能できる。庭園にある三重塔「圓通閣」は登録有形文化財であり、旧寛永寺の五重塔、池上本門寺の五重塔とともに、東京に残る三古塔の一つである。この塔の景色だけ見ていると、どこか地方の山の中にでもいるような錯覚を覚える。6月の宵には、ここで蛍も見られる。

Chinzanso was built on land that was considered ideally suited for camellias to grow naturally. Former Prime Minister Yamagata Aritomo first built his residence here in 1878. It was converted to a hotel with banquet facilities in the mid-1900s, and has come to be known as the Hotel Chinzanso Tokyo, welcoming elite international guests and hosting global conferences. In the gardens that have cleverly incorporated hills and dales, each of Japan's four seasons is well represented by cherry blossoms in the spring, fresh green foliage in summer, jewel-like colors in autumn, and camellias in winter. The three-story pagoda (*Entsukaku*), a Registered Tangible Cultural Property, is one of the three oldest structures of its kind to remain standing in Tokyo. The other two pagodas are located at Kaneiji Temple in Ueno and at Honmonji Temple in Ikegami. Gazing at this pagoda can take your mind away to the remote mountainside. In June, fireflies dance around the entire garden.

四谷 Yotsuya

　四谷は、仕事の行き帰りによく通る街である。道幅が広くて緑も多く、歩いても、車で走っても心地良い。迎賓館赤坂離宮や江戸城外堀跡、須賀神社、於岩稲荷などの名所もある。於岩稲荷は役者がよく訪れる社である。鍵を抱える狐像と宝珠を抱える狐像が、本殿前で参拝者を迎える。私が参拝した時、祖父に手を引かれた2、3歳くらいの幼子が、柔らかな日差しの中で、2人揃ってお稲荷さんに手を合わせていた。日々の慌ただしい生活の中で「祈る」とか「感謝する」といった心や行為が忘れられがちな昨今、二人の後ろ姿に、ほほえましさと美しさを感じた。

I pass through Yotsuya often on my way to and from work. The roads are wide, there are many trees, and it is a pleasant town for a walk as much as it is for driving through. There are several notable sites: the Akasaka Palace; the outer moat to Edo Castle; Suga Shrine; and the Oiwa Inari Shrine, which is frequently visited by actors. A pair of foxes in front–one with a lock, the other with a gemstone–welcome visitors. When I was there to make an offering, I watched a toddler and an elderly gentleman (his grandfather, perhaps) walk up to the shrine, hand in hand. Swathed in a soft light, they put their hands together in prayer to the *inari* gods. We are so busy all the time, we tend to forget to bow our heads, or to be grateful. As I watched them walk away, I could not help but smile at the goodness of it.

刻を見つめて　Staring at Time

於岩稲荷は道をはさんで2つの社がある。於岩稲荷陽運寺は悪運断ちや、煙草・酒との縁切りを祈願する人々も訪れるという。縁切りには、悪縁を切り、正しい縁を結ぶ「縁結び」という意味がある。於岩稲荷田宮神社は参拝者のために御札が用意され、心に響く言葉が記されている。

Oiwa Inari is a name that is also attached to the Younji Temple next door to the Oiwa Inari Tamiya Shrine. Visit the Oiwa Inari Younji Temple for help with severing a relationship you no longer want. That includes a string of bad luck or your dependence on cigarettes or alcohol. The end of a bad relationship makes room for a better one (good fortune and better health, for instance). Such meaningful words are written in the blessings (*ofuda*) from Oiwa Inari Tamiya Shrine.

なじみの街角
That Familiar Place

ふだん急いでいる時は街の景色にあまり目を向けないものだが、気持ちに余裕があると、風にそよぐ街路樹や、空の色が目に入る。「たまには僕たちのいる景色にも気を留めてよ」と、呼びかけられているように思える時がある。

Usually, I am in such a hurry that I do not pay much attention to city views. When I stop to take notice, I rediscover such things like the color of the sky, trees swaying in the breeze. They're calling out to me, "Look my way once in a while!"

花園のさくら Hanazono Cherry

新宿区屈指のパワースポットと称される神社。商売繁盛、厄除開運、仕事運向上のご利益あり。境内にある芸能浅間神社は自分磨きの神様。芸事成就、才能開花にご利益がある。

This shrine is the highest rated power spot in Shinjuku. It blesses business prosperity, career advancement and protects from evil. On the right hand side within the shrine complex, the god for self-improvement at Geino Asama Jinja will bless the arts and help develop talent.

新宿 Shinjuku

　新宿の繁華街・歌舞伎町の近くに、その昔、たくさんの花が咲き乱れる美しい花園があったという。徳川御三家筆頭の尾張藩下屋敷の庭の一部。その由縁で、この地の神社が「花園稲荷神社」と名づけられたのだとか。現在の正式名称は花園神社。ここは舞台役者の野外舞台の聖地でもあり（野外舞台の代名詞になっている神社はなかなか珍しい）、この境内でしばしば開催されてきたテント芝居（仮設のテント小屋）は、多くの傑作を生んできた。11月には恒例行事の酉の市が立つ。春には朱塗りの社殿に、満開の桜が美しく映える。花園の桜には、不思議と静かな華やぎがある。特に夜桜は、繁華街の近くとは思えない落ち着いた風情を感じることができる。

Once upon a time, there was a field full of beautiful flowers (*hanazono*) near Shinjuku's Kabukicho entertainment district. It was part of the suburban estate belonging to the Owari family, the most prestigious of the three branches of the Tokugawa clan. Hanazono Shrine was named after that field of flowers. This shrine is also holy ground for stage actors. For some years now, tents are periodically set up for a temporary stage. The events have given birth to some of the best plays. The Cock Festival takes place in November. In spring, the cherry blossoms in full bloom beautifully complement the shrine's bright vermillion paint. The Hanazono cherry has a mystical and serene beauty about it. Especially after dark, the night blossoms offer a respite from lively Kabukicho.

ドコモタワー Docomo Tower

　新しい建物に絵心をそそられる時がある。2000年、JR代々木駅近くに背高のっぽのドコモタワーができてから、絵の構図にタワーを入れる楽しみが増えた。ニューヨークのエンパイアステートビルを思わせるこのビルは周囲の風景と調和し、絵全体を引き立ててくれる。この周辺は東京の都心部でありながら、公園や緑地に恵まれた地域でもある。ドコモタワーをランドマークにぐるりと歩いてみれば、高層ビルがひしめく大都会の風景とはまた違った、東京の別の表情が見えてくるかもしれない。

There are times when a new building can pull you into a new phase of subjects. Ever since the tall and lanky Docomo Tower was constructed near Yoyogi train station in 2000, I started to include towers in my art compositions. Docomo Tower has the look of New York's Empire State Building. It seems to fit well within its surroundings, and it complements the entire frame of my sketches. This area is the city center, but it also has parks and green spaces. If you walk around in a circle, keeping Docomo Tower in your sight, you might see a different side of Tokyo unlike the typical cityscape of skyscrapers.

代々木駅 Yoyogi Station

ドコモタワー
Docomo Tower

JR山手線 Yamanote Line

首都高速4号新宿線 Shuto Exp. No. 4

冬の晴れ間に（代々木公園）
In the Winter Sun (Yoyogi Park)

代々木公園は季節ごとに広葉樹が色彩を美しく変え、いつ行っても飽きることがない。森の向こうに見える新宿副都心のビル群は、ニューヨークの街並みのようだ。

Yoyogi Park has many broad-leafed trees that show off beautiful color changes; never a dull moment. The cluster of skyscrapers beyond the forest reminds me of New York.

なごり秋（新宿御苑）
Fall Everlasting (Shinjuku Gyoen)

新宿御苑の芝生の広場から見上げるドコモタワー。木々が緑の頃。色づき始めた頃。そして冬枯れの木立が透けてみえる頃。同じ場所でも季節ごとの絵を描きたい時があって、この眺めは何枚も描いてきた。

Looking up at Docomo Tower from the lawn at Shinjuku Gyoen here. Sometimes I like to make seasonal drawings of the same place. I have drawn several pieces of this view: when the leaves are full, when their tips turn color, and when you can see through the bare trees in winter.

都会の森（原宿） Urban Forest (Harajuku)

JR原宿駅のクラシックな駅舎越しに見えるドコモタワー。その手前は明治神宮の森である。都会の真ん中のこの大きな森が、大正時代に作られた人工の森だとは、意外に知らない人も多いだろう。

Docomo Tower stands out behind the vintage-style Harajuku train station. Shown in front is the forest at Meiji Shrine. Not many people are aware that it did not exist before 1912, when volunteers planted some 100,000 trees to create the shrine forest.

原宿駅 Harajuku Station

秋色さんぽ（千駄ヶ谷駅近く）
Autumn Color Walk (Sendagaya)

車でここを通るたびに、いつか描きたいと思っていた景色だった。いちょうの木が色づいて、今日こそはの思いで描いた。すぐ近くに、2020年オリンピックの会場予定地である国立競技場跡地（新国立競技場）や東京体育館がある。

I wanted to draw this view every time I drove by. The day I saw that the gingko leaves had turned golden, it was now or never. Part of the Summer Olympic Games in 2020 will be held at the National Stadium and Tokyo Gymnasium nearby.

明治神宮 Meiji Shrine

　明治神宮は、代々木上原にある私のギャラリーから近いこともあって、よく散歩にでかける場所である。好きな時間帯は朝の早い時分か、昼下がりの頃。季節を問わず、特に午後の日差しの中で、大きな木々がゆったりと光り輝いて見える瞬間が好きである。ここでは散歩のついでに、おみくじを引くことにしている。明治神宮のおみくじは吉凶を占うのではなく、明治天皇がお詠みになった歌が一首書いてあるのだが、不思議とその時々の心情にあった歌を引き当てる。その一首で、妙に気持ちが落ち着くことがよくある。

Meiji Shrine is close enough to my art gallery in Yoyogi Uehara that I can take frequent walks there. I like to go early in the morning or right after noon. No matter what season, there is a certain time of day when these giant trees shine gloriously in the afternoon sun. I love that moment. And I make it a point to draw a blessing (*omikuji*) on these walks. Instead of fortunes, *omikuji* at Meiji Shrine are classical poems that were written by the Emperor Meiji. For some strange reason, the poem always describes how I feel at that moment. Words can be a source of comfort at times.

午後の栄光　Afternoon Glory

明治神宮の森閑とした木立に囲まれると、都心にいることを忘れてしまう。近年、参拝すると運気が上がるパワースポットとしても有名になり、参拝者が絶えない。JR原宿駅、地下鉄明治神宮前駅から行くのが便利。

Being surrounded by the peaceful forest at Meiji Shrine makes me forget that I am in the heart of Tokyo. Conveniently accessible from Harajuku train station or Meiji Jingumae metro stop, in recent years, this busy shrine has become one of the most popular power spots in Japan, a place for spiritual and mystical immersion.

黄金色の路 The Golden Path

通りの両側に約150本のいちょうの木が植えられている。青山通り口から絵画館に向かって背の高い木から順に植えられていて、遠近法が活用されることによって美しい眺めになっている。絵画館の周囲にサイクリングコースもあり、自転車をレンタルできる。

About 150 tall gingko trees are planted on both sides of the street. Beginning at Aoyama Dori, the trees are planted in order of height as they continue toward the Gallery. The perspective view created by this deliberate landscape design is absolutely gorgeous. Rent a bicycle and circle the path around the Gallery.

神宮外苑いちょう並木 Gaien Gingkos

　東京にも自然に親しむ場所はたくさんあるが、神宮外苑のいちょう並木は格別だ。青山通り口から約300メートルにわたって続く二重並木のいちょうの木々が、秋には燃えるような黄金色に染まる。見頃の11月にはいちょう祭りが開催され、路上は落ち葉で埋まり、黄色いじゅうたんの上を歩いている気分になる。いちょう並木の先には、幕末明治の歴史的絵画が展示された聖徳記念絵画館と、複数のスポーツ施設がある。ゴルフ練習場、アイススケート場、テニスクラブ、バッティングセンター、フットサルコートなどがあり、気軽にスポーツを楽しめる。

There are many places in Tokyo where you can commune with nature, but the streets lined with gingko trees at Jingu Gaien are exceptional. The double rows of gingkos continue for 300 meters starting from Aoyama Dori into the park. In the fall, they turn flaming gold. The Gingko Festival takes place during the best time to see these beauties, in November, when the leaves fall to the ground and create a soft golden carpet under foot. Past the gingko trees, the Meiji Memorial Picture Gallery (*Seitoku Kinenkan*) exhibits masterpieces from the Meiji Era. A number of sports facilities are available for the public's enjoyment: a driving range, a skating rink, tennis courts, a batting cage and futsal courts.

恵比寿ガーデンプレイス
Yebisu Garden Place

　JR恵比寿駅東口からスカイウオークを5分ほど歩くと、デパート、オフィス、ビアホール、フランス料理店、ホテルなどが建つ恵比寿ガーデンプレイスに着く。さりげない景色の中で、1本の街灯や、枯れた一枝が目に留まる。どこか懐かしく感じるのは、かつてこの地にあった煉瓦造りのビール工場を思い出させるからだろうか(1988年までここはビール工場だった)。敷地内にはミニシアターや東京都写真美術館があり、近隣に落ち着きのあるバーやレストランも多い。大人が楽しむに事欠かない街と言えるだろう。

Just five minutes on the Skywalk from Ebisu train station's East Exit takes you to Yebisu Garden Place, a mixed-use complex of offices, a department store, a beer hall, French restaurants and a hotel. In this casual atmosphere, the artist in me is charmed by the sight of a single lamppost and a bare branch. Something feels familiar; must be the brick building that was once a brewery (they made beer right here until 1988). A mini-theatre and the Tokyo Metropolitan Museum of Photography are located within the complex. Nearby, there are quite a few quiet bars and restaurants. This is a town for grown-ups.

憩いのひととき　A Moment of Respite

「恵比寿」の地名は「ヱビスビール」に由来する。ヱビスビールは日本のプレミアムビールのひとつだ。恵比寿ガーデンプレイスの正面にそびえるこの赤煉瓦造りの建物はビアホール、敷地内にはビール記念館もある。

The town of Ebisu was named after the Yebisu beer label, one of the two premium beers of Japan. This brick building is now the beer hall. There is also a beer museum within the complex.

都会の冬空
Winter Sky in the City

恵比寿は都内どこにでもアクセスがよく、誰もが住んでみたい街の上位に名を連ねる。この都会的な風情の中で、樹木は春夏秋冬を重ねている。

Conveniently located to major points in the city, Ebisu is one of the top-ranking neighborhoods in Tokyo where people seek to live. Even in this urban atmosphere, the trees and shrubbery can maintain their beauty through the seasons.

春の香(中目黒)
The Fragrance of Spring

毎年、桜が咲く1週間ほどの間、目黒川の両岸は人、人、また人である。満開の桜も見ごたえがあるが、散った花びらが川面いっぱいに浮くさまもいい。

Every year, during the week that the cherry blossoms are in bloom, there are people, people, people everwhere on the banks. Full blooms are beautiful; so are the petals that float on the water like a blanket.

目黒川 Meguro River

　JR目黒駅から行人坂を下ると、目黒川に架かる太鼓橋に出る。ここから中目黒、池尻大橋に向かって両岸に、約4kmにわたる桜並木がある。春になると川沿いに長いアーチを描くように、桜の花が咲き誇る。木々は年々大きさを増して、咲き方も華やかになっているようだ。この周辺には私も気に入った喫茶が何軒かあって、よく散歩に訪れる。桜並木の四季の変化を楽しみながら、気が向くと、いつも通る橋から見慣れた景色に筆を走らせる。桜が終わると、みずみずしい新緑の季節、そして秋の落葉の季節もいい。

目黒川散歩(中目黒) A Stroll Along the River

三宿から品川へと続く目黒川。川沿いに遊歩道が続き、おしゃれなカフェや雑貨店などがある。8月には中目黒で夏祭りが開催され、阿波踊り、よさこいなどダイナミックな踊りが見られる。

Heading downhill on Gyoninzaka from Meguro train station, you reach Taiko Bridge (*Taiko-bashi*) over Meguro River. For about four kilometers, from here to Naka Meguro toward Ikejiri Ohashi, the banks are lined with cherry trees. In the spring, cascading branches form a wide arch of cherry blossoms over the river. The trees grow bigger and bigger each year to form even more splendid blooms. I take frequent walks around here, stopping in at some of my favorite coffee shops. I can watch the cherry trees change with the seasons and easily start sketching the familiar view from the same bridge whenever it strikes me. When the cherry blossoms fade, it is time for young sprouts, and soon, autumn.

Meguro River runs from Mishuku to Shinagawa. Fashionable cafes and variety stores can be found along the riverwalk. Nakameguro hosts a summer festival in August. Dance teams put on energetic performances as they parade down the street doing traditional dance steps to modern music.

West
of Tokyo

　新宿から山梨、長野を通って名古屋へ通じる中央本線。この沿線には古くからの名所名跡や秘境がたくさんある。目まぐるしく変わりゆく景色の中で、時代や場所を超えて変わらぬものを目にした時の安堵感。偉大な芸術家たる自然を前にすると、人を芸術家呼ばわりしても、しょせんは自然が創った造形美の模倣に過ぎないとさえ思えてくる。

The Chuo Line is one of the major trunk lines in Japan, providing rail service between Shinjuku-Yamanashi-Nagano and on to Nagoya. Many historical sites, famous places and secret hideaways have long existed along the Chuo. As the landscape changes at a bewildering pace, to see something that transcends time and location can provide a sense of stability. An artist can easily be humbled by the realization that we are only creating synthetic imitations of beauty when compared to Nature, the greatest artist of all.

吉祥寺 Kichijoji
秋川渓谷 Akigawa Gorge
小金井 Koganei
立川 Tachikawa
中央線 Chuo Line
勝沼 Katsunuma
河口湖 Lake Kawaguchi

吉祥寺 Kichijoji

　吉祥寺の北口から吉祥寺サンロード商店街を少し歩いたところに、雲洞山月窓寺という禅寺がある。人々を迎え入れる山門は、一風変わった門である。大陸からの流れをくんでいるのであろうが、その文明の伝わりを思うと、歴史も描く楽しみの一つになる。境内では1986年から幽玄の世界、吉祥寺薪能が演じられている。坐禅はもとより、「動く禅」である合気道の道場もある。この大都会の中で、神社・仏閣は昔から変わらぬ街のオアシスであり、人々の心のオアシスである。

A short walk from the Sun Road shopping arcade, just outside the North Exit of Kichijoji train station, Gessoji Temple welcomes visitors with an unusual entryway. The shape of the gate to this Zen temple suggests there were architectural influences from the Asian continent. When I consider how civilization spreads, the privilege of drawing a piece of history adds another layer of enjoyment. Since 1986, *Noh* plays have been performed in the evenings under the light of bonfires (*takigi Noh*). Besides offering *zazen* training, Gessoji also has a *dojo* for *aikido*, the art of "moving *zen*." Shrines and temples are havens in this megalopolis of Tokyo, a sanctuary for the soul.

街のオアシス
（吉祥寺 雲洞山月窓寺）
Sanctuary

月窓寺は多摩八十八ヶ所霊場1番である安養寺、たんす地蔵で知られる光専寺、厄除け日蓮の蓮乗寺とともに、吉祥寺の「四軒寺」と称される。

Anyoji Temple (the first stop on the Tama 88 Temple Pilgrimage), Kosenji Temple (home of the bureau god, *tansu jizo*), Renjoji Temple (houses a statue of Priest Nichiren that expels evil) and Gessoji Temple are clustered together and therefore known as the Kichijoji Four.

小金井・立川 Koganei & Tachikawa

　武蔵小金井駅から小金井街道を少し歩くと、住宅地の中に鬱蒼とした森が見えてくる。菅原道真公の徳を敬い、社殿が造られたとされる小金井神社。その一角には弓道場があり、私が絵を描いているところまで、ビシッと的を射る張詰めた音が聞こえてくる。日本の伝統的な武道は神社・仏閣に良く似合う。同じく中央本線沿線の立川には、立川水天宮 阿豆佐味天神社がある。大きくはない社だが、この風格のある本殿に魅せられる。日本の多くの神社・仏閣は、昔から同じ場所に変わらぬ姿で存在する。目まぐるしく変わりゆく都会の景色の中で、変わらぬものを目にするひとときは、自分を癒してくれる瞬間でもある。

As you walk along Musashi Koganei Kaido from Musashi Koganei train station, a thick forest tucked within a neighborhood of homes starts to appear. Here, Koganei Shrine was built in honor of Sugawara Michizane, a brilliant scholar from the Heian Period who was deified as the god of education. In a corner of the compound is an archery *dojo*. I can hear the arrows go "thump" as they hit their targets, all the way to where I am making a sketch. Japanese martial arts fit nicely in the shrine setting. On the same Chuo Line is Tachikawa, site of the Azusamiten Shrine, otherwise known as Tachikawa Suitengu. Although it is not a big place, the main building is attractive for all its character. Many Japanese temples and shrines exist just as they were when they were first built. In a hectic and ever changing urban environment, the sight of something constant can offer a moment of sweet respite.

夏のなごり（小金井 小金井神社）
Lingering Summer

小金井神社は病気平癒、正直を守る神、文学・書道芸能の神、学問の神のご利益あり。境内には全国唯一の臼供養の石臼塚がある。

Visitors to Koganei Shrine seek blessings for honesty, literature, calligraphy, academics and to recover from illness. There is a pile of millstones in the shrine, the only "boneyard" in Japan for this once common household item.

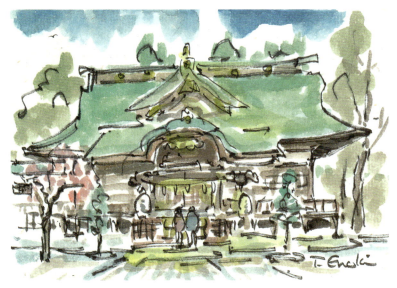

春の日差し
（立川 阿豆佐味天神社）
In the Spring Sun

阿豆佐味天神社に祀られているのは、少彦名命、天児屋根命のお二柱。医薬・健康・知恵の神、文学・芸術の神のご利益があると言われている。猫返し神社とも称され、境内には「ただいま猫」の石像あり。

Two princes from Japanese mythology are worshipped at the Azusamiten Shrine in Tachikawa: *Sukunahiko no Mikoto* as the protector god of medicine, health and wisdom; *Amenokoyane no Mikoto* as the protector of literature and the arts. There are several smaller shrines on the premises, each offering a different blessing. One of them is dedicated to protecting cats.

鍾乳洞の主
Odake Caverns

小さな赤い橋を渡って鍾乳洞へ。その周辺には深緑におおわれた爽やかな風景が広がっている。

Cross a quaint little red bridge to reach the caverns. The area is surrounded by a refreshing green landscape.

初夏の渓谷
The Gorge in Early Summer

新緑、紅葉など、四季折々に自然を愛でる楽しみがある。6月初旬に鮎釣りが解禁されると、秋川は釣り人で賑わう。

Spring blooms and fall foliage are among the beauties of nature to enjoy year round. Anglers flock to Akigawa River for sweetfish (*ayu*) as soon as the season opens in June.

秋川渓谷 Akigawa Gorge

　初めて秋川渓谷を訪ねた時、「東京にもこんなにホッとする場所があったんだ」というのが、私の素直な感想であった。この渓谷には「大岳鍾乳洞」という、あまり知られていない地下の世界がある。鍾乳洞に入ってみると、全長300mの美しい洞窟が広がっていた。七色に輝く乳石や、長い歳月をかけて形造られた鍾乳石の美しさに心を奪われる。ちょっと足を延ばせば、都会の喧騒を忘れさせてくれる自然美がある。こんな身近なところに未知の世界があることを、もっと多くの人に知ってほしいと思う。

How could a place in Tokyo provide such a sense of relief? That was my honest impression the first time I visited Akigawa Gorge. There is a little known subterranean world here called the Odake Caverns. Inside, ceilings are as high as 300m. It is breathtakingly beautiful: crystals refracting in all colors of the rainbow; mineral deposits that took years and years to form. All you have to do is venture out a little to escape the commotion in the city. I wish more people would get to know such a place.

勝沼 Katsunuma

　ぶどうや桃、ワインの産地として知られる勝沼は、JR新宿駅から中央線特急で約2時間。東京からの日帰り旅ができる地域である。車があれば中央自動車道の勝沼ICで降りると便利だが、私はむしろすいている一般道を通りながら、車窓に広がる果物畑を眺めるほうが気に入っている。7月頃から11月上旬にはぶどう狩りが、11月3日のボジョレーヌーボー解禁日以降は、町内のワイナリーで作られた新酒ワインを味わえる。近年、この地で醸造される甲州ワインは、海外でも高い評価を得ているという。甲州ワインビーフや甲斐サーモン、ワインに合いそうな地元の食材や郷土料理も豊富だ。

Grapes and peaches grow everywhere in Katsunuma wine country. The two-hour train ride from Shinjuku Station on the Chuo Line super express is an easy day trip. By car, you can head toward the Katsunuma exit on the Chuo Expressway, but I prefer taking less congested local roads that wind through different towns, enjoying the views of orchards along the way. You can pick your own grapes starting in July through early November. Once Beaujolais Nouveau is released on November 3, the wineries in town bring out their latest vintage for tasting. The Koshu wine produced in this region has been internationally recognized in recent years. Regional foods like Koshu Wine Beef and Kai Salmon are a couple of excellent choices for local wine pairings.

ぶどうの街並み
Grape Town

勝沼には観光ぶどう園が100軒くらい、ワイナリーが30軒くらいある。ぶどう狩りのシーズンには、道の左右におびただしい数の観光農園の看板が立つ。

There are around 100 vineyards and 30 wineries in Katsunuma. During picking season, signs to draw in tourists swarm the roadside.

たわわな稔り
Bountiful Harvest

果物の中で一番好きなものは？　私は迷わず「ぶどう」である。秋の収穫期、たわわに実る勝沼のぶどう畑は、ぶどう好きにはたまらなく嬉しい景色だ。もし庭つきの家に住んだら、私もぶどうの木を植えて、秋に庭のぶどう棚を見渡したい。そんな夢はあるものの、いまだ実現していない。

If I were asked, what is your favorite fruit? I would have to say, GRAPES! When the orchards in Katsunuma are laden with grapes during harvest season, what a spectacular sight it is for a grape-lover! If I had a yard, I would definitely plant grapevines so I can have my own vineyard. Someday...

逆さ富士 Mt. Fuji Reflected

富士五湖の中でも河口湖は逆さ富士の名所である。湖面にくっきりと映し出される逆さ富士を見るなら、晴天で風が少なく湖面の波が穏やかな日がいい。湖北ビューライン沿いの広いエリアで湖面が見える。

Among the Fuji Five Lakes, Kawaguchi is the most famous for the reflection of Mt. Fuji in the lake (*Sakasa Fuji*). For best views of this double beauty, pick a clear day with low winds and barely lapping waves. The Kohoku View Line on the North side of the lake has a long stretch of good lake views.

河口湖 Lake Kawaguchi

　河口湖畔から見た「逆さ富士」である。葛飾北斎を筆頭に、これまでたくさんの画家や写真家、作家がこの風景を表現してきたが、季節やその日の天候、湖面の波模様、さらに表現者の心模様によって富士の姿は様々に変化する。おそらく同じものは二つとないだろう、それが逆さ富士の魅力であり、奥深さなのだと思う。近頃は河口湖畔に富士山ライブカメラが設置され、いつでもどこからでも河口湖の景色がインターネットで見られるようになったという。それはそれで便利なのだが、有史以来続くこの見事な景色は、やはり一度は自分の目で見ておきたいものだ。

This is *Mt. Fuji Reflected*, viewed from the shores of Lake Kawaguchi. Hokusai leads a long list of painters, photographers and writers who have captured this view. Depending on the season, the weather, the lake's wave patterns, or even the artist's sentiment of the moment, Mt. Fuji can look very different. There are no two alike, and to me, that makes Mt. Fuji so enchanting and profound. Today there are live camera feeds on line that allow you to view Lake Kawaguchi on the internet, anytime, anywhere. That's convenient, too, but this fantastic sight deserves to be seen in person at least once in a lifetime.

South
of Tokyo

　江戸時代、品川から京都に通じていた東海道と並ぶように、東海道本線と東海道新幹線が走っている。この沿線にある街は街道文化の影響か、それぞれに独特の歴史を育んでいるように思う。何百年も続く街では、かつての面影を探しながら歩くといい。道端に見つけた小さな史跡や、頬に触れる心地良い風に、心がふとタイムスリップするだろう。

During the Edo Period, the Tokaido Road connected Shinagawa and Kyoto. Today, the Tokaido Main Line and the bullet train (*shinkansen*) trace over that same path. Towns along this rail line were heavily influenced by highway culture. Each town seems to have developed from an independent background of its own. Some of these towns are rich with hundreds of years of history. Walk through them in search of how they might have looked in the past. The sight of a small monument by the roadside or the wind softly brushing against your cheek just might trigger a fleeting moment of slipping into a different time.

野毛 Noge
大井ふ頭 Oi Pier
多摩川 Tama River
横浜 Yokohama
北鎌倉 Kita-Kamakura
鎌倉 Kamakura
日本平 Nihondaira

不思議空間（善養寺）Mystic Spaces

本堂の前に門番のように立つ石像と数々のユニークな石像は、見て歩くだけで愉快だ。善養寺は京都の智積院が総本山。境内には樹齢700〜800年と言われるカヤのご神木がある。寺の隣は六所神社。この町を守る二社なのであわせて散策したい。

A statue appearing to guard the main building is one of several unique stone figures throughout the compound. Have fun with them. Also look for the sacred nutmeg yew tree (*kaya*) that is more than 700 years old. Zenyoji Temple falls under the head temple of Chishaku-in in Kyoto. Next door is Rokusho Shrine, the other protector of this town.

野毛 Noge

　世田谷の野毛にある「善養寺」は、一度訪れて忘れ得ぬ印象を持った寺だ。赤い橋を渡ると、本堂に至る参道や境内に亀や河童（カッパ）などの石像や置物が、いくつもいくつも並んでいる。ふだん訪れている寺の静謐なイメージとは異なる、そこはまるで不思議空間。大陸からの伝来か、1体1体の石像がとてもユニークなのだ。人の心は弱いものだから、英雄、偉人、伝説の動物たちを神様に仕立ててあやかりたい気持ちはよくわかる。だが仕立てられた本人は、自分が神様になろうと思って生きたわけではないだろう。日本に神社仏閣は約15万カ所あるというから、知る人のみぞ知る空間は、まだまだたくさんあるのかもしれない。

I went to Zenjoji Temple in Noge (Setagaya) just once. It was very unusual and left quite a lasting impression. After I crossed a red bridge to enter the temple grounds, I passed by some interesting figures carved out of stone. Statuaries of a turtle (*kame*) and a troll (*kappa*) guided the way to the main building (*honden*), setting off a different feel from the customary serenity of most temples. Each statue was unique, some suggesting Chinese influences. Perhaps we seek strength from prayer, so I can see how heroes, great men, and mythical creatures get turned into icons of worship. But the ones who were deified probably did not set out to become a god from the beginning. There are about 150,000 temples and shrines in Japan. There must be many more spaces like this that are known only to those in the know.

多摩川大橋 Tama Ohashi

多摩川大橋緑地から眺める多摩川大橋。橋の上を国道1号線が通り、東京と神奈川を結ぶ主要道路になっている（橋の途中に県境がある）。ブルーのアーチの橋は送電専用橋。河川敷から眺めると、並行する二つの橋が重なって見える。

Here is Tama River Bridge (*Tamagawa Ohashi*) as it appears from the green spaces on the banks. Route 1 is a major road that runs across the bridge to connect Tokyo and Kanagawa. The prefectural border is in the middle of the bridge. The blue arch is dedicated to power lines. From the banks, the two seem to overlap.

多摩川 Tama River

　多摩川は、隅田川とともに東京を代表する川である。多摩川周辺はかつて「多麻」と呼ばれ、江戸時代には多摩川上流から水を引き、人々の生活用水が確保された。現在は川辺の広いエリアが緑地化され、公園や憩いの場が作られている。野球、サッカー、ゴルフ、バーベキュー、サイクリング、ジョギング、犬の散歩など、いろいろなレジャーが楽しめる。川辺は爽やかな風が吹き、見晴らしが良い。河川敷から眺める夕陽はとても美しい。晴天の休日を過ごすには最適の環境だ。心地良い風が、スケッチする筆の運びを後押ししてくれる。

Like Sumida River, Tama River is one of Tokyo's major waterways. It was a primary water source for the capital during the Edo Period. Today, a long stretch of the riverbed has been converted into green spaces for parks and recreation. A range of leisurely activities and facilities for baseball, soccer, golf, cycling, jogging, dog walking, and picnic areas with barbecue pits are available. Soft breezes blow on the river banks and the views are great. What a great place to spend the day off. The gentle puffs of wind push along the pencil in my hand to help me with my sketches.

大井ふ頭 Oi Pier

　品川から南のシーサイドには、京浜運河に沿って、海や運河を望める公園がいくつか点在している。その中で私が気に入っているのが大井ふ頭中央海浜公園だ。ここには「なぎさの森」という水辺の緑地があって、広々とした緑の中を野鳥や蝶が飛び、人々がバードウォッチングや磯遊びを楽しめるようになっている。私はたまたま湾岸の道を車で走っていた折に見つけたのだが、出逢った景色に新鮮さを覚えて車を脇道に止め、絵を描いた（こんな時のために、車にはいつもスケッチ道具を積んでいる）。水と緑、空の構図はやはり心を和ませる。この森の景色は、東京モノレールの車窓からも目にすることができる。

On the shoreline south of Shinagawa, parks along the Keihin Canal offer great ocean and canal views. My favorite spot is the seaside park at Oi Pier (*Oi Futo Kaihin Koen*). There is a forest by the shore called *Nagisa no Mori*, a sanctuary for wild birds and butterflies where you can enjoy birdwatching and beachcombing. I stumbled upon this place when I stopped to take in the landscape while I was driving along the coastline. I parked on a side road and started to sketch the water, trees and sky, a composition that brings harmony to body, mind and soul. (I always keep a sketch pad in the car just for times like this.) You can also see this view if you ride the Tokyo Monorail.

なぎさの森　Forest Shores

広大な公園には野球場やバーベキューエリアもあり、運河に沿った遊歩道から夕焼けがきれいに見える。東京モノレールの大井競馬場前駅近く。東京シティ競馬のナイトレース、定期的に開催される東京シティフリーマーケットもおもしろい。

This is a spacious park with baseball fields and barbecue areas, and sunset views from the walking path along the canal. Near *Oi Keibajo Mae* station on the Tokyo Monorail. The Tokyo City Flea Market (held several times a month) and night-time horse racing at Ohi Race Track are other attractions.

横浜 The Bluff at Yokohama

夜景や中華街で人気の横浜。海を見渡せる小高い丘に、港の見える丘公園がある。展望台から横浜ベイブリッジや横浜港が一望できる。眼下に広がる風景に魅せられながら、ふと150年以上前の開港当時の景観を想像してみた。近代的なビルも橋もなかった頃、やはり今と同じような心地良い海風が吹いていたに違いない。道を隔てて隣にある外人墓地には、海外から赴いてこの地に骨をうずめた多くの人々が眠る。園内はローズガーデンでもあり、110種1300株ものバラが咲く。風に揺れる花びらが、眠る人々をなぐさめてくれているかのようだ。

Yokohama is a popular place for night views and Chinatown. On The Bluff overlooking the sea is Harbor View Park (*Minato-no-Mieru Oka Koen*). You can see Yokohama Harbor and Yokohama Bay Bridge from the observatory. Captivated by the view spread before me, I tried to imagine how it must have looked a century and a half ago when the port first opened. There were no skyscrapers, no bridges back then, yet the soft ocean breezes must have felt the same. The Yokohama Foreign General Cemetery (*Gaijin Bochi*) across the street is the final resting place for those who came to this country from abroad to stay forever. In the rose garden, there are more than 110 cultivars among the 1,300 rose bushes. Sometimes their petals quiver in the breeze as if to comfort the departed.

バラの季節 Roses in Bloom

バラが咲くのは春と秋の2回。バラの開花時期以外にも桜、あじさい、クリスマスローズなど四季折々の花が咲く。

Roses bloom twice a year in the spring and in fall at Gaijin Bochi. In addition, cherry blossoms, hydrangeas and Hellebores (Christmas and Lenten roses) decorate the different seasons.

港の風(港の見える丘公園) Harbor Breezes

関東屈指の観光スポットである。周辺の博物館、資料館めぐりも楽しい。疲れたら洋館の一軒家カフェでお茶を一杯。

Harbor View Park is a top-ranking tourist spot in the Kanto area. Get in tune with history at the museums and libraries around the park. Break for a cup of tea at one of the European style coffee houses and pastry shops.

歴史のおもかげ Traces of History

北鎌倉駅から鎌倉街道沿いに小さな川が流れている。昔はどじょうやうなぎもとれたそうだ。山の方に進むと、鎌倉幕府が山を掘削して作った切通し（交通路）が残っている。

Starting at Kita-Kamakura train station, a creek runs along Kamakura Kaido, where people once fished for loaches and eels. Toward the mountains, part of the road system created by the Kamakura Bakufu still exists. Paths were cut deep into the hillside.

トンネルを抜けて（東慶寺）Through the Tunnel

北鎌倉駅に近い東慶寺。紫陽花、水仙、花菖蒲、梅など四季の花が咲く。かつて縁切寺として知られた寺。江戸時代、離婚を望んでも叶わなかった女性がこの寺に駆け込み、3年修行すれば自由を手にすることができたという。明治時代後期までは男子禁制の尼寺であったが、現在は禅寺であり、誰でも拝観できる。

Hydrangeas, daffodils, plum blossoms and lotus flowers bloom in season at Tokeiji Temple near Kita-Kitamakura train station. During the Edo Period, a woman whose husband would not grant her a divorce could be released from the marriage if she could manage to enter the temple and spend three years in prayer and study. Today, the former nunnery that was active until the early 1900s is a Zen temple open to the general public.

北鎌倉 Kita-Kamakura

　鎌倉幕府以来、800年の歴史を持つ鎌倉は、三方を山に囲まれ、もう一方は海という地形を生かして街が作られた。鎌倉時代の街並みは、外敵が進入しにくい要塞のようであったという。この街を散歩する時は、古都の面影を探しながら歩くといい。北鎌倉には、円覚寺、東慶寺、浄智寺、明月院など、北条時代の寺院が点在する。いずれも紫陽花の名所。横須賀線の両側に紫陽花の花が咲く頃、電車を入れ込んだ花の写真を撮りに、多くの人が訪れる。私が絵を描くのもそうだが、人には美しいものや、珍しい景色を、絵や写真におさめたくなる傾向があるようだ。

Kamakura has an 800-year history that goes back to the time when it was the former seat of the first shogunate government (*bakufu*). Strategically surrounded by mountains and the sea, the de facto capital (1185-1333) was well postured to stave off enemy aggression. When you take a walk in this town, look for traces of the old capital. Enkakuji, Tokeiji, Jochiji and Meigetsuin Temples in Kita-Kamakura were built during the Hojo Era, all famous for hydrangeas. In late June, when the hydrangeas are in full bloom along the tracks of the Yokosuka Line, crowds rush over to snap pictures of the train framed by flowers. I think people are inclined to preserve beautiful or unusual landscapes on canvas and film. The same can be said for me.

鎌倉 Kamakura

　鎌倉の鶴岡八幡宮は武家政権を築いた源氏の氏神とされ、日本を代表する八幡宮の一つとして知られる。春には何百本もの桜の木が湘南の太陽の光を浴びて、いっせいに開花する。湘南の顔として人々に親しまれ、常に参拝者が絶えないこの神社が、桜見物をかねてますます活気づく。また、鎌倉市内には山裾や道の端に、昔ながらの小さな石塔や石仏が数多く残る。庚申塔は、60年に1度巡ってくる庚申の日に神仏を祀る行事から、各地の村々で建てられた守り神。市内に数百基あると言われている。

Tsurugaoka Hachiman Shrine is the family shrine of the Minamoto clan, the first samurai family to assume governing power from the aristocracy by establishing a military government. It is one of the representative *hachiman* shrines in Japan. In the spring, the blossoms of hundreds of cherry trees glisten in the Shonan oceanside sun, putting on a big show. Already a well-visited site, the shrine buzzes with even more activity than usual with cherry blossom viewers. An interesting object to look for in Kamakura is the *koshinto*, which are stone statuaries that were erected by villagers every 60 years. There are hundreds of them in Kamakura alone. *Koshinto* originated from the Tao-based folklore of the three pests (*sanshi*) that reported on our behavior to the Emperor in Heaven every 60 days while we slept. Bad behavior was punishable by sudden death in extreme cases. For spiritual protection, villagers built *koshinto* monuments in the year of *Kanoe Saru* according to the ancient Chinese astrological calendar of *Jikkan*. The next cycle for *Kanoe Saru* wlll come in 2040.

庚申塔と紫陽花
Koshinto and Hydrangeas

雨風にさらされながら人々を守ってきた庚申塔。ふだんは見過ごしがちだが、紫陽花の季節には花の色で石像が際立って見える。

These protective monuments have withstood the elements for years; yet hardly noticed until the hydrangeas bloom and help them stand out.

春が来た　Spring is here!

若宮大路の二の鳥居近く、「茶寮いの上」の2階から見た景色。桜の花のピンク色と赤い鳥居のコントラストが見事。段葛と呼ばれる桜並木の参道が、春にその素晴らしい色合いを見せてくれる。

From a second floor tea room (*Saryo Inoue*) near Ni no Torii on Wakamiya Oji Street, the pink cherry blossoms are beautiful against the red *torii* gates. Such a magnificent display of spring color graces Dankazura, the long walkway leading up to the shrine.

日本晴れ Under the Sun

日本平は標高約300ｍの丘陵地。富士山、清水の街並み、茶畑、三保松原、駿河湾が一望できる。近隣の茶畑では、4月中旬から10月までお茶摘み体験ができる。ロープウェイで久能山に登れば、家康ゆかりの久能山東照宮がある。

At elevation 300m above sea level, Nihondaira is on a plain in the middle of hill country. Mt. Fuji, Shimizu City, tea fields, Miho Matsubara and Suruga Bay can be viewed in one sweep. Pick your own tea leaves from April to October in the tea fields nearby. Take the cable car on the ropeway to the top of Mt. Kuno (*Kunozan*) and visit the burial site of Tokugawa Ieyasu (1543-1616) at Kunozan Toshogu Shrine.

日本平 Nihondaira

　昔から数多くの絵描き達がこの山を描き、多くの傑作、駄作が生まれてきた。富士山を真正面に望める日本平は、日本を代表する名所の一つと言えるだろう。正確に言えば東海地方なのだが、東京駅から新幹線で1時間あまり、どうしてもこの景色は本書に加えたかった。これからも多くの人々の絵や写真の素材になるであろうことを思えば、やはりこの山は日本一の山である。

Over the years, so many artists have created masterpieces and mistakes portraying this mountain. The head-on view of Mt. Fuji from Nihondaira is one of the most famous sites in all Japan. It is actually located in the Tokai Region, but because it is just an hour's ride from Tokyo on the bullet train, I just had to include this landscape in the book. No doubt Mt. Fuji will continue to be a subject for more artists and photographers. Mt. Fuji, after all, is Japan's premier mount.

East
of Tokyo

　総武本線に乗って東へ進むと、東京には意外と多くの川があり、多くの橋が架かっていることに驚かされる。人はそれらの川や橋を使って物資を運び、多くの街を発展させてきた。総武本線は千葉を過ぎると、房総半島を迂回しながら太平洋岸の銚子へと向かう。そこにはかつて水運や漁業に支えられてきた、太平洋岸独特の街の面影が色濃く残る。

Going East on the Sobu Line, it surprises me to find so many rivers and bridges in Tokyo. They were essential to moving goods and supplies, and many towns flourished as a result. After passing Chiba, the train follows the Boso Peninsula toward the Pacific coast and Choshi. There are still elements distinct to the coastal region remaining in these towns once supported by seaside industries such as water transport and fishing.

北千住 Kita-Senju

北千住は、江戸時代に日光街道の宿場町として栄えた街である。駅を降りて西に行けば隅田川、東に行けば荒川と、二つの川を見渡せる場所にある。駅は5路線が乗り入れる大きなターミナルになっているが、散歩すると江戸時代から変わらぬ道幅の商店街があったり、蔵や宿場の名残がある。人は歴史を見る目が備わると、街や古い建物を見る目も変わってくる。そのあかしに、街中にある今も人が暮らす民家が、貴重な文化財に思えてきたりもする。

Kita-Senju developed as a stopover on Nikko Road (*Nikko Kaido*) during the Edo Period. From the train station, Sumidagawa lies to the West and Arakawa lies to the East so you can look across both rivers from the same spot. The train station itself is a large, modern terminus that serves five different lines. By contrast, the town is a vestige of the Edo Period. The streets in the shopping area are still as narrow, and remnants of the original storehouses and old inns can still be found. Gaining an understanding for history can change the way we look at old towns and buildings. The older homes in town, for instance, appear as though they should be important cultural assets.

川面を渡る風（千住大橋）
Winds Across the River

隅田川にかかる千住大橋は、江戸入りした徳川家康が隅田川に初めて架けた橋である。当時、この地は日光街道の千住宿で、江戸の入口として旅人が多く行き交った。松尾芭蕉の奥の細道の旅も、ここから始まったという。当時の橋のようすを記した絵や解説が、橋のたもとに掲げられている。

When Tokugawa Ieyasu became Shogun and moved the capital to Edo, Senju Ohashi was the first bridge he built across Sumida River. At the time, Senju was a crosspoint for travelers entering and leaving the capital via Nikko Kaido. Haiku poet Matsuo Basho started his tour of the remote provinces here and later published the famous travelogue, *Oku no Hosomichi* (1694). Pictures and inscriptions at the foot of the bridge tell the way things were around then.

蔵の街 The Old Storehouse

宿場の街 The Old Inn

千住宿は、東海道品川宿、中山道板橋宿、甲州街道内藤新宿と並んで江戸四宿の一つ。町にはかつて商家や問屋、旅籠屋、蔵だった建物が残り、往時がしのばれる。その造りが立派だったり、風格があるとなおさら。かつての街道の賑やかさを想像するのが楽しくなる。

During the Edo Period, there were four main overnight stopovers (*juku*) for travelers using the major roads: Shinagawa on the Tokaido, Itabashi on the Nakasendo, Naito Shinjuku on the Koshu Kaido and Senju on the Nikko Kaido. The sight of some of the older buildings in town can prompt a yearning for the past, especially when they boast great craftsmanship and architectural details. These were once busy mercantile shops, wholesalers, taverns and warehouses. Imagine how lively these streets must have been with all the flurry back then!

柴又 Shibamata

　街を散歩していると、それぞれの街で、その街の顔とも言うべき神社に出逢う。初めて柴又を訪れた時、この神社がそうなのだと思った。昭和の時代に生まれ育った日本人になじみの深い映画『男はつらいよ』シリーズで、いつも語られ、登場している神社である。映画で見慣れているせいか、初めて来たにもかかわらず境内の風景に身近な親しみを覚える。人の感覚は不思議なものである。本堂手前に、瑞龍松がどっしりと枝を広げている。よくぞここまで枝を伸ばしてきたものだ。長い歳月、世代を超えた人々が、松の成長に合わせて枝の支柱を作ってきたのであろう。そんな地元の人々のやさしさに感じ入る光景である。

On my walks, sometimes I encounter a shrine that can be said to represent its town. The face of the town, so to speak. I thought of this shrine in that vein the first time I visited Shibamata. You see, my generation grew up during the Showa Era watching *Otoko wa Tsurai yo*, a series of movies about *Tora san*, a roving peddler who hails from Shibamata. Taishakuten Shrine appears in every one of those movies when *Tora san* longingly recounts his home to the people he meets in distant places. I felt like I already knew the shrine since I had seen it so many times on film. In front of the main hall is a black pine tree whose horizontal branches are spread long and wide to create the image of a dragon. It is an amazing sight, the result of great care taken by many generations in shaping those branches over the years. The dragon tree is a spectacle that emanates the compassion of the townspeople.

瑞龍松　The Dragon Tree

瑞龍松は、龍のように天に昇る樹の形が特徴の松である。江戸時代からこの地にあって、樹齢約500年と言われている。

This black pine is shaped in the form of a dragon climbing toward the heavens. Believed to be almost 500 years old, the dragon tree (*zuiryu matsu*) appears in artwork from the Edo Period.

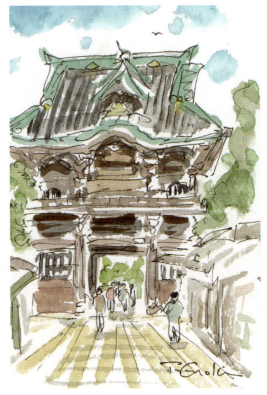

柴又の顔（柴又帝釈天）
Face of the Town

参道の突きあたりの二天門。素木造の質素な造りだが、細部に精巧な浮き彫りの装飾彫刻が施されている。参道には名物のだんご屋やせんべい屋、老舗の川魚料理店などが並ぶ。

At the end of the main path (*sando*) to Shibamata Taishakuten is a gate with two gods enshrined on either side of the passageway (*Nitenmon*). It is a simple structure made of unfinished wood, yet the carvings and architectural elements are very detailed. Rice sweets (*dango*) and rice crackers (*senbei*) are famous local favorites sold along the *sando*. Restaurants here specialize in freshwater fish.

やなぎはらすいこう
柳原水閘 Yanagihara Floodgates

この一帯は、江戸時代に水田や畑として開拓されたが、川の氾濫による被害が多く、明治時代に柳原水閘が建設された。近代の希少な土木遺産で、経済産業省の近代化産業遺産に指定されている。

This area experienced frequent flooding once it was developed into rice fields and farm land during the Edo Period. The Yanagihara flood gates, built in 1904 to control the raging river, have been designated as part of Japan's Heritage of Industrial Modernization by the Ministry of Economy Trade and Industry.

松戸 Matsudo

柴又帝釈天の裏手にある江戸川河川敷から、都内に唯一残る渡し船が出ている。これが小説や歌にも登場する「矢切の渡し」だ。船頭さんが手で漕ぐ船で、乗船時間は約5分。川の途中に東京と千葉の県境があって、向こう岸に松戸の街並みが広がっている。この近く、柳原親水広場の中に「柳原水閘」というレンガ造りの水門が残っている。明治時代に流域の水田の用水量を調整する役目を果たし、江戸川の氾濫から人々を守った。その秘めたる面影を、ひっそりと静かに今に残している。

コスモス Cosmos Flowers

秋になると、江戸川の河川敷にコスモスが咲く。「江戸川松戸フラワーライン」という名のお花畑。松戸の人々がボランティアで大切に育てているという。

In the fall, cosmos flowers take over the Edogawa riverbanks. The flower fields (*Edogawa-Matsudo Flower Line*) are maintained by volunteer Matsudo residents.

The Yagiri ferry crossing (*Yagiri no watashi*), touted in story and song, is the only remaining hand-rowed ferry boat (*watashi bune*) in Tokyo. The ferry departs from the Edogawa riverbed behind Taishakuten Shrine in Shibamata, crosses the prefectural boundary for Tokyo in the middle of the river and in just five minutes, lands on the other side in Chiba where city views of Matsudo fan out. Tucked away in a nearby park (*Yanagihara Shinsui Hiroba*), flood gates faced in brick (*Yanagihara Suiko*) are a quiet reminder of the past. Built during the Meiji Period, they once played an important role in controlling Edo River.

成田 Narita

　成田空港のすぐ近くに、「成田山のお不動さま」として知られる成田山新勝寺がある。ここは940年に開山し、1000年以上の歴史を持つ寺院。歌舞伎の成田屋（市川團十郎家）とゆかりの深い寺である。JR成田駅か京成成田駅に降りるとすぐ参道があり、両脇に食べ物屋や土産店が軒を連ねて賑やかだ。境内には大本堂をはじめ、約300年前に建立された幾つかの御堂がある。御護摩の祈祷や写経、坐禅、断食修行も行なえる。とりわけ大晦日から元旦にかけては大変な人出で、初詣には約300万人が訪れる。日本人にはたいして信心深くなくても、正月のお詣りは欠かせない人が多いと思う。かくいう私もその一人だが、人ごみは大変だと思いながらも、年頭の思いを新たにしたくなる国民性なのだと思う。

Right by Narita Airport is a temple complex that has a history of more than a thousand years. Founded in the AD 940, Naritasan Shinshoji Temple is affectionately known as Narita's *Ofudosama*. It is also the sanctum for *kabuki* actors of a guild (*Naritaya*) named after Naritasan by founder Ichikawa Danjuro I. Just steps from Narita train station, the approach to the temple (*sando*) is a hopping neighborhood of old-fashioned shops selling foods and souvenirs. In addition to the Great Main Hall, there are a number of auxiliary buildings within the temple complex, some dating back to the 1700s. Naritasan offers group and private sessions for *Goma* Prayer rituals, copying Buddhist sutras by hand to boost the mind and spirit, *zazen* training, and the ascetic practice of supervised fasting (*danjiki shugyo*). More than three million people visit the temple for First Prayer (*hatsumode*) for the new year beginning New Year's Eve. *Hatsumode* is an important ritual for most Japanese people, even if we are not deeply religious, even for me. We know there will be a crowd, but it does not stop us from starting out the new year with a clean slate. Must be our national character...

懐かしの参道　A Memorable Path

門前町として賑わってきた成田山の表参道には、ひと時代前の建物が多く残っている。昔の日本に思いを馳せたい時にはもってこいの道で、絵心をかきたてる道でもある。「うなぎ」と書かれたのぼりが多い。江戸時代、成田詣でが盛んな頃に、長い旅の疲れを癒すために、栄養のあるうなぎ料理がふるまわれたそうだ。

Along the *sando* is the heart of the temple town. Most of the shops are examples of older architecture, and it is the perfect place for me to slip into the past. It also makes me want to pull out my sketch pad. Banners advertising eel (*unagi*) are a testament to Naritasan's enduring popularity since the Edo Period, when travelers treated themselves to a quick energy meal of *unagi* after a long journey on their pilgrimage.

青空の中へ　Into the Blue

参道から急な石段を上った先の小高い丘に伽藍が立つ。青空に突き刺さるような堂々たるいでたち。信仰を寄せる人々の思いも、青空の中をまっすぐに突き進むがよい。

Gallantly standing on a small hill above the steep stone steps at the end of the *sando*, the Great Peace Pagoda seems to pierce the skies. For all those who come to worship, may the skies part for the prayers to be thrust into the heavens!

冬に吠える
Howling at Winter

犬吠埼は太平洋を一望でき、灯台近くの海沿いに見晴らし抜群の温泉もある。日本で一番早く初日の出を見ることができる場所。日の入りが見たければ、銚子市内の小高い丘にある「地球の丸く見える丘展望館」へ。

An uninterrupted view of the Pacific horizon can be seen from Inubosaki. For fantastic ocean views, try the seaside hot springs (*onsen*) near the lighthouse. Japan's earliest sunrise greets Inubosaki every morning. To watch the sun rise, visit the Ocean View Observatory in Choshi.

銚子 Choshi

銚子半島の最東端にある犬吠埼灯台は、明治時代に造られて140年以上も風雪に耐えてきた灯台で、世界灯台100選に選ばれている。断崖絶壁にそそり立つ美しいフォルムの白亜の塔は、英国人による設計。灯台下で荒波が断崖の岩礁に砕けるさまは、雄大そのものだ。これを見るには穏やかな天候より、冬場の悪天候の方が似合う気がする。岬から市内に入ると、港町・外川が広がる。港に向かって8つの坂道が並行し、それぞれの坂道に歴史の名残りがある。路地の所々に残る古い家屋や石垣の風情もいい。

坂のある街
Hill Town

海に続く坂道に、昔ながらの港町の佇まいが残っている。犬吠埼、外川へはチャーミングなローカル電車・銚子電鉄で。始発の銚子駅から終点の外川駅まで、10駅約20分。1時間に1〜2本運行している。

Hills leading into the ocean are filled with vintage landscapes. Inubosaki and Tokawa can be reached by Choshi Railways, a charming country railroad that runs once or twice during the hour. It takes 20 minutes to cover all ten stops.

Positioned at the easternmost tip of Choshi Peninsula, the Inubosaki Lighthouse has survived more than 140 years of harsh sea weather since its construction during the Meiji Period. It was selected by the International Association of Lighthouse Authorities as one of the world's top 100 architecturally well-designed examples. Looming over a precipice that drops straight into the ocean, a British architect designed the white tower in beautiful form during the late 1800s. Imagine this picture on a monumental scale: huge waves crashing into the cliffs, rocks drenched with seaspray. It might make a better picture on a bad day in winter than it would on a nice sunny day. As you leave the cape, the hilly harbortown of Tokawa starts to spread out. There are eight streets that run parallel to each other toward the harbor, each with a little secret history of its own. Older homes and stone walls dot the alleyways and turn the atmosphere cozy.

佐原 Sawara

　1960年代から今日にかけて、各地の開発によって歴史のある街道や昔ながらの街並みがいくつも消えていったが、佐原（千葉県香取市）はそんな時代の影響をまぬがれた、数少ない場所である。伊能忠敬旧宅、佐原三菱館、蕎麦で知られる小堀屋本店、江戸時代創業の福新呉服店など、由緒ある老舗が並ぶ。また佐原は、潮来（茨城県潮来市）、鹿嶋（茨城県鹿嶋市）と並んで、千葉と茨城にまたがる水郷三都として知られる。水運業に支えられた頃の面影が色濃く残る水路もあり、川面の懐かしい風情が広がっている。

Beginning in the 1960s, many of the historic roads and hometowns in Japan lost their vintage charm due to zoning and development. Sawara is one of the few places that was not ruined by modernization. Start at the visitors' center, which used to be the Mitsubishi Bank. Browse through Shobundo book store, shop at the Fukujin kimono shop, have lunch at Koboriya noodle shop, and visit the house of Ino Tadataka, whose first exact Map of Japan was the result of surveying the entire country on foot for 17 years. Sawara, Itako and Kashima are known as the three cities forming the historic waterway district (*suigo*) straddling Chiba and Ibaragi Prefectures. Traces of a once busy water route supported by the canal system are still evident in the nostalgic landscape.

なつかしの街 Down Memory Lane

何百年も前から続く商家では、当時の人々の愛用品や衣装、生活道具を見ることができる。

Period clothing and artifacts are on exhibit in the merchant houses that have been around for hundreds of years.

あやめの季節 Iris Blooming

佐原から潮来、鹿嶋にかけての一帯は、あやめや花菖蒲の里である。毎年5、6月には紫や白、黄色のあやめが咲き誇る。

From May to June, over a million Japanese irises bloom in purple, white and yellow throughout Sawara, Itako and Kashima.

華やかなりし思い出
Exquisite Memory

佐原には「佐原まちぐるみ博物館」という看板が掲げられた店が約40軒ある。江戸から大正時代にかけての店構えが多く残り、それぞれ見学できる。

About 40 shops in Sawara participate in the town's open museum (*Sawara Machigurumi Hakubutsukan*). Many storefronts are from the Edo to Taisho Periods. Visitors are welcome to take a look.

水路の街 Water Town

佐原へは成田空港からJRで1時間弱。町中を流れる小野川沿いでは、船に乗って江戸風情のある景色を巡ることができる。

Sawara is less than an hour's train ride from Narita Airport. To tour the untouched Old Edo landscape, cruise the Ono River running right through town.

North
of Tokyo

　東京駅を出発して北へ向かう新幹線は、今や6路線ある（東北、上越、山形、秋田、北陸、北海道）。ふと思い立って旅する時も、新幹線のおかげで昔なら考えられないほど遠くへ行けるようになった。軽井沢、前橋、那須、いずれも小旅行におすすめの場所である。近年は川越の評判が良く、蔵造りの街並みを着物姿で歩く観光客が多いと聞く。

The *shinkansen* now has six branches heading North from Tokyo Station: Tohoku, Joetsu, Yamagata, Akita, Hokuriku and Hokkaido Lines. Even when I decide at the last minute to take a trip, I can go to far off locations unimaginable in the past, thanks to high speed trains. For a short trip, I recommend Karuizawa, Maebashi, or Nasu. In recent years, Kawagoe has become extremely popular. I hear tourists can walk around for the day clad in a rented kimono and truly enjoy the atmosphere of the old town styled in storehouse architecture (*kura zukuri*).

川越 Kawagoe

　小江戸・川越の魅力は、蔵造り建築や時の鐘をはじめとする貴重な文化財が、今も人々の営みの中にあることだ。重厚な開き扉や堅牢な瓦屋根、明治時代の川越大火にも耐えてきた街並みに、小江戸商人の心意気が伝わってくる。路地を見上げれば、川越のシンボル「時の鐘」が、長い歴史を経て時を刻み続けている。もし私がいつか時代劇を撮れる時代村を創るとしたら、時の鐘はぜひ創ろうと思う。

Koedo Kawagoe is full of charm and character. In the old town district, impressive storehouse style architecture (*kura zukuri*) and the bell tower (*Toki no Kane*) are important cultural properties that remain an integral part of business as usual. Architectural elements such as grand entryways, massive doors and substantial roof shingles avoided complete destruction in the Great Fire of 1893 while the rest of Kawagoe was engulfed in flames. Their survival embodies the Koedo merchant's determined disposition. Looking up, I see that the symbolic *Toki no Kane* continues to keep time for the town's long history. If I ever had the chance to build a set for historical movies, I would definitely include that bell tower.

時の鐘　The Bell Tower

時の鐘は、江戸時代前期に建てられた川越のシンボル。電柱も電線もないスッキリとした景観がいい。文明の利器は時として懐かしい景色の邪魔になるものだ。

Toki no Kane has been Kawagoe's symbol since it was originally built in the early 1600s. The line of sight is clear without overhead electrical wires to obstruct the view. The benefits of technological advancement can interfere with a good landscape, but here, neither telephone poles nor electrical lines clutter the view.

懐かしの街並み　Old Town, Revisited

川越の蔵造りの街並みは、「重要伝統的建造物群保存地区」や「美しい日本の歴史的風土100選」に指定されている。色とりどりのガラスが散りばめられた石畳、菓子屋横丁に日本らしい風情が残る。1918年に建築された埼玉りそな銀行（旧第八十五銀行本店本館）や、1928年築、古代ギリシャ・ドリス式の列柱が印象的な川越商工会議所（旧武州銀行川越支店）は一見の価値あり。

The Kawagoe storehouse district was designated as an Important Preservation District for Groups of Historical Buildings. It is also known as one of the 100 Most Beautiful Historical Scenes of Japan. The stone walk embedded with multi-colored glass beads in Penny Candy Alley (*Kashiya Yokocho*) is reminiscent of a bygone era. Saitama Risona Bank occupies a building from 1918. The Kawagoe Chamber of Commerce operates out a former bank built in 1928; the stately Doric columns are worth a look-see.

水辺の情景 The Brook

深い緑と澄んだ水。軽井沢の静寂は、日本の自然の美しさを再確認させてくれる。

Deep greens, clear waters. The peace and tranquility at Karuizawa reaffirms the beauty of nature in Japan.

軽井沢 Karuizawa

　軽井沢に行くと、都会では感じられない澄んだ空気と静寂を実感する。私がよく歩く散歩道に好きな情景があって、「あのベランダから見下ろすと、清流の中に白い小さな水中花が咲いているのかなあ」などと、住んでもいないのに想像して楽しんでいる。水辺の景色が、いつも心を癒してくれるのだ。散歩の途中で寄った喫茶店で、庭にあったひと房を思わず描きたくなった。絵は衝動を感じた瞬間が、描き時である。訪れるたびに、描きたい気持ちにさせてくれる。それが軽井沢という場所の持っているパワーかもしれない。

When I go to Karuizawa, the air is crystal clear and it is quiet all around. Can't find that in the city. I like to stop at my favorite spot on the walking path I often take and ponder, "If I were to look down from that deck, would I see small white flowers growing in the brook? Are they aquatic flowers?" It's not even my house, but I can still have a little fun with imagination. Water in any landscape soothes me. I stop at a tea house, and I find myself sketching the single cluster of redcurrants (*fusasuguri*) in the garden. Drawing is impulsive. It's all about seizing that very moment you feel something. Every time I go to Karuizawa, it makes me want to create. This place has a special power over me.

ふさすぐり Redcurrants

高原に自生している草花は、派手さはなくともほっこりとしたかわいさがある。

Wildflowers growing in the highlands may not have quite the pizzazz, but they certainly are cute and fluffy little things.

前橋 Maebashi

　川好きの私が、群馬で気に入っているのが、前橋市街を南東へ流れる広瀬川である。かつて江戸との間で物資などを運ぶ水運で栄えた。萩原朔太郎の詩に詠まれた文学情緒あふれる川でもある。春の桜の香り、夏の涼しげな柳、川面に映える冬のイルミネーション、一年を通して様々な表情を見せてくれる。せせらぎを聞きながら、ゆっくりと川沿いを散歩すると、遊歩道の枝垂柳が柔らかな風にそよぐ。なんとも日本情緒を感じる景色だ。

I love rivers. My favorite one in Gunma Prefecture flows southeasterly through the city of Maebashi. Hirose River, once a busy water route for transporting goods to and from the old capital of Edo, was also made famous by none other than Maebashi's own Hagiwara Sakutaro (1886-1942), the father of Japanese free verse poetry. The scent of cherry blossoms in spring give way to the cooling sway of the willow branches in the summer, then the lighted trees reflect on the water's surface in winter. Every season has a different expression. Take a slow-paced walk along the river bank with the sound of running water in the background and weeping willows billowing in the gentle wind.....how *Japonesque*.

柳に風 Willows in the Wind

柳の新芽が芽吹く頃、川面を渡る風は優しさを増し、絵にも爽やかさが加わる。広瀬川にかかる朔太郎橋から眺める夜桜もいい。河畔には文学館や朔太郎像もある。

When the willow trees start to bud, the winds blowing across the river become more gentle, adding more life to my drawings. Cherry blossoms at night from the Sakutaro Bridge look pretty good. Also check out the riverside library and statue of the bridge's namesake poet.

那須塩原 Nasu-Shiobara

東京から那須塩原まで新幹線で約1時間。那須は避暑やリゾートでゆったりと時間を過ごすのもいいが、ふと思い立って旅に行けるエリアでもある。那須連山のふもとにある那須温泉郷と塩原温泉郷は、ともに1000年以上の歴史を持つ温泉郷。山あいの川沿いに建つ温泉街は全国至るところにあり、この構図はいかにも定番であるが、だからこそ安心感もある佇まいだ。那須高原では熱気球がさかんで、これが今、地元を活気づけているようだ。巨大な風船は人を乗せ、爽やかな風にのって夢を運ぶ。高原の風は、夢の散歩道の水先案内人である。

Spending a well-planned vacation at Nasu-Shiobara hot springs resort is well worth the trip. It is only about an hour from Tokyo on the bullet train (*shinkansen*), so it is also close enough to get away on the spur of the moment. There are several hot springs (*onsen*) at the foot of the Nasu mountain range and more in the Shiobara Onsen Village. Both *onsen* resorts were discovered more than a thousand years ago. A riverside *onsen* village sitting on the slopes of a mountain is a common landscape, but the fact that it looks typically Japanese makes it authentic. Hot air balloon rides are the now thing to do in the Nasu Highlands (*Nasu Kogen*), and the ballooning business is helping the local economy thrive. Huge balloons lift off from the wide green fields carrying voyagers, flying up, up and away into the blue skies, riding the highland winds, guiding the path to their dreams.

青空散歩 A Walk in the Sky

西那須野塩原インター近くにある那須千本松牧場で、熱気球が体験できる。大空高く昇る熱気球から、那須高原の360°大パノラマを眺められる。

Venture out on a hot air balloon ride and take in 360-degree panoramic views of Nasu Highlands at Nasu Senbonmatsu Farm located near the Nishi Nasuno Shiobara Exit on the Tohoku Expressway.

**温泉の街
Onsen Village**

塩原温泉郷は平安時代に発見され、昔から『塩原十一湯』と呼ばれて人々に親しまれてきた。約150の源泉があり、豊富な湯量と多彩な泉質を誇る。

When the hot springs at Shiobara were discovered during the Heian Period (794-1185), they were called the 11 Springs of Shiobara (*Shiobara Juichiyu*). About 150 geothermal springs provide a generous supply of natural hot water with healing mineral properties.

| A Few Words |

私にとって、演じることも、絵を描くことも、古武術や乗馬も、表現活動の一環です。近年、科学技術の進歩によって、人は地球の主人であり、自然は利用するものと大きな勘違いをしてしまいました。奇跡の星地球の美しさと、人は自然に生かされていることを、これらの絵を通じて伝えられればと思います。

We have made great strides in the advancement of science and technology in recent years. Along the way, we have mistakenly made ourselves masters of the Earth, gravely misunderstanding that Nature is there for the taking. This miracle planet of ours is beautiful, and Nature is our source for life. I am hoping that my paintings—and through various forms of expressive art, whether I am acting, drawing, horseback riding or practicing the ancient martial arts of Japan—can show that we should not abuse the Earth's bounty.

| Galleries |

日本国内に4ヵ所、東京、北海道、大分、鹿児島に榎木孝明のギャラリーがあります。各ギャラリーで、ご当地の風景画や原画、画集、書籍、アートグッズなどを展示販売。

The author's original art, publications and art pieces are on exhibit and available for purchase at his galleries in Tokyo, Hokkaido, Oita and Kagoshima.

北海道 美瑛 Biei, Hokkaido

西美の杜美術館「榎木孝明 水彩画館」
Takaaki Enoki House of Water Colors

TEL: 0166-95-2339
http://biei-art.jp/

自然豊かな美瑛にある美術館。美瑛を描いた作品をはじめ国内外の風景作品が常設展示されています。

北海道上川郡美瑛町字ルベシベ第二
開館日時：4月末〜10月末の9:00〜16:00（入館は15:30まで）
水曜日休（祝祭日の場合は翌平日休）、11月1日〜4月中旬は休館

In a nature rich environment, this museum features local landscapes of Biei and those of Japan and the world.

No. 2 Rubeshibe, Biei-cho Aza, Kamigawa-gun, Hokkaido
Open Late April to October 9:00-16:00. Closed for winter and on Wednesdays. Closed Thursday also if a Holiday falls on Wednesday.

東京 代々木上原 Yoyogi Uehara, Tokyo

アートスペース クオーレ
Cuore, an ArtSpace

TEL: 03-3460-8100
http://www.officetaka.co.jp/gallery/index.shtml

Cuore（クオーレ）とはイタリア語で心という意味です。ここでしか見られない作品を展示販売しております。ほっと一息つける癒しの空間です。

東京都渋谷区上原1-35-7 KUDOビル1F
開館日時：12:30〜18:30　土・日・祝祭日休

Artwork and items on display or for purchase at Cuore (it means "heart" in Italian) are available only at this gallery. Please stop by for a relaxing experience.

First Floor, Kudo Bldg., 1-35-7 Uehara, Shibuya-ku, Tokyo
Open M-F 12:30-18:30. Closed Holidays.

大分 飯田高原 Handa Highlands, Oita

榎木孝明 美術館 Takaaki Enoki Art Museum

TEL: 0973-73-3812
http://www.e-kyushu-geijutsu.com/

飯田高原の「九州芸術の杜」の中にある美術館です。大分をはじめ、各国各地の風景画を常時100点展示。

大分県玖珠郡九重町田野1712-707
開館日時：10:00〜17:00（入館は16:00まで）
休館日はお問い合わせください。

More than 100 landscapes of Oita, Japan and other parts of the world are on regular exhibit at this gallery where nature abounds in Handa Highlands. The gallery is located within Kyushu Geijutsu no Mori art park.

1712-707 Tano, Kokonoe-machi, Kusu-gun, Oita Prefecture
Open 10:00 -17:00. Please call to confirm we are open for the day of your visit.

鹿児島 菱刈町 Hishikaricho, Kagoshima

榎木孝明アートカフェ「ギャラリーひしかり」
Enoki Takaaki Art Cafe Gallerie Hishikari

TEL: 0995-26-0230

榎木孝明の故郷にあるアートカフェ。アートグッズや作品を展示。

鹿児島県伊佐市菱刈川北2876-1
開館日時：9:00〜18:00（日曜日・祝祭日は17:00まで）　第3日曜日、年末年始休

This art cafe located in the artist's hometown displays artwork and related items.

2876-1 Hishikari Kawakita, Isa-shi, Kagoshima Prefecture   Open M-Sa 9:00-18:00, Su 9:00-17:00. Closed third Sunday of the month and New Year holidays.

榎木孝明 Enoki Takaaki

1956年生まれ。武蔵野美術大学デザイン科に学んだのち、劇団四季に入団。1981年、『オンディーヌ』で初主演。1983年劇団四季を退団し、翌年のNHK朝の連続テレビ小説『ロマンス』の主演でテレビデビュー。以後、映画『天と地と』、プロデュース主演映画『半次郎』、映画テレビ『浅見光彦シリーズ』、NHK大河ドラマ、舞台などで活躍。旅と絵を好み、世界の風景を描き続けている。

Enoki Takaaki was born January 5, 1956, in Kagoshima, Japan. He studied at Musashino Art University before joining the Shiki Theatre Company and making his debut as a stage actor in *Ondine* (1981). He left the Company in 1983, and first appeared on TV playing the lead role in NHK's Morning Drama Series *Romance* (1984). He has pursued an active career since, starring in a number of successful productions: in the 1990 epic film *Ten to Chi to* (*Heaven and Earth*); in the *Asami Mitsuhide Series* TV murder mystery as the title role crime-solver; in the weekly NHK historical fiction drama series; and in various theatre productions. In 2010, Enoki produced and starred in *Hanjiro*. Fulfilling a passion for both art and travel, Enoki paints landscapes of the places he visits.

コルーチィ・ステラ Stella Colucci

東京に生まれ育つ。米国・州立大学政治学部、大学院博士課程卒。翻訳家、クロス・カルチャーコンサルタントとして、日本と海外を結ぶ様々なプロジェクトを手がける。近訳に『Walking TOKYO』『Walking KYOTO』。

Stella was born and raised in Tokyo. She studied at Sophia University International College, then earned her BA in Political Science and a Masters in Public Administration from US State universities. Stella has worked on various projects to promote relations between Japan and abroad throughout her career as a translator, writer, business executive and cross-cultural consultant. Her most recent publications are *Walking TOKYO* and *Walking KYOTO*.

編　集	Takashi Kanazawa (ANNOVA)
	岸川麻美、加藤愛子、一宮晴美、良本淳子
デザイン	参画社
編集協力	オフィス・タカ、山本美智代、Mark Bond, Amy Martinez

Artfully Walking
TOKYO AND BEYOND
榎木孝明と歩く関東名所

2016年6月8日　　第1版第1刷発行
2016年6月19日　　第1版第2刷発行

著　者	榎木孝明
訳　者	コルーチィ・ステラ
発行者	木村由加子
発行所	まむかいブックスギャラリー 
	〒108-0023　東京都港区芝浦3-14-19-6F
	TEL.050-3555-7335　www.mamukai.com

Paintings and text copyright ©2016 by Enoki Takaaki
Translation copyright ©2016 by Stella Colucci
All rights reserved.

Printed in Japan
ISBN 978-4-904402-07-8　C0095

＊落丁、乱丁本はお取り替え致します。
＊本書の一部あるいは全部を無断で複写複製することは法律で認められた場合を除き、著作権侵害となります。